Ageing and the Elderly

Series Editor: Cara Acred

Volume 239

Independence Educational Publishers

First published by Independence Educational Publishers

The Studio, High Green

Great Shelford

Cambridge CB22 5EG

England

© Independence 2013

Copyright

Photocopy licence

British Library Cataloguing in Publication Data

Ageing and the elderly. -- (Issues ; v. 239)

1. Aging--Social aspects.

I. Series II. Acred, Cara.

362.6-dc23

ISBN-13: 9781861686374

Printed in Great Britain

MWL Print Group Ltd

Contents

Introduction

Ageing and the Elderly is Volume 239 the **ISSUES** series. The aim of the series is to offer current, diverse information about important issues in our world, from a UK perspective.

ABOUT AGEING AND THE ELDERLY

The number of people aged 60 and over has doubled since 1980. There are now more people in the UK aged 60 and above than there are under 18, and by the year 2050 the number of 80-year-olds in the UK will have quadrupled. With this in mind, issues such as age discrimination, age-related health concerns and the cost of ageing are essential topics for discussion. Should we embrace our ageing population? What needs to be done to improve quality of life for older people in the UK? This book will guide you through the spectrum of issues associated with ageing, exploring the challenges our ageing population faces now and in the future.

OUR SOURCES

Titles in the **ISSUES** series are designed to function as educational resource books, providing a balanced overview of a specific subject.

The information in our books is comprised of facts, articles and opinions from many different sources, including:

- Newspaper reports and opinion pieces
- Website fact sheets
- Magazine and journal articles
- Statistics and surveys
- Government reports
- Literature from special interest groups

A NOTE ON CRITICAL EVALUATION

Because the information reprinted here is from a number of different sources, readers should bear in mind the origin of the text and whether the source is likely to have a particular bias when presenting information (or when conducting their research). It is hoped that, as you read about the many aspects of the issues explored in this book, you will critically evaluate the information presented.

It is important that you decide whether you are being presented with facts or opinions. Does the writer give a biased or unbiased report? If an opinion is being expressed, do you agree with the writer? Is there potential bias to the 'facts' or statistics behind an article?

ASSIGNMENTS

In the back of this book, you will find a selection of assignments designed to help you engage with the articles you have been reading and to explore your own opinions. Some tasks will take longer than others and there is a mixture of design, writing and research based activities that you can complete alone or in a group.

FURTHER RESEARCH

At the end of each article we have listed its source and a website that you can visit if you would like to conduct your own research. Please remember to critically evaluate any sources that you consult and consider whether the information you are viewing is accurate and unbiased.

What is ageing?

Information from the Science Museum.

What is ageing?

Your body wears out as you get older. Scientists are trying to find out why this happens by investigating what happens to the body's cells as they age.

How long will you live?

The lives of our Stone Age ancestors were dangerous, and short. As recently as a century ago, the average life span in the UK was only 49 years for men, and 52 for women. Many children died before the age of five. Today, thanks to steady improvements in diet, healthcare and living conditions, the average life span has risen to over 77 for men and nearly 82 for women.

Who's the oldest?

The longest life on record is that of Jeanne Calment, who was 122 years old when she died in 1997. Shirechiyo Izumi of Japan was thought by many to be the world's oldest man when he died aged 120 in 1986, although his age has been disputed. Elsewhere in the world there have been unconfirmed reports of people living even longer.

Will you live to reach 100?

British citizens who live to see their 100th birthdays receive a telegram from the monarch. More people than ever are living a 100-year life. In 1952, the Queen sent out just 255 centenary telegrams, but in 1999 she sent over 3,500. A long life seems to run in the family – if your mother reaches 100 you are more likely to live to celebrate your 100th birthday too.

What happens as you age?

As you get older, your skin wrinkles because it becomes thinner and less elastic. It gets drier too as it makes less oil and sweat. Your bones become more visible as you store less fat beneath your skin. Inside the body your bones and muscle become weaker. Your memory gets worse, and your immune system cannot fight disease as easily.

What makes you age?

Your body is made up of around 100 million million cells. Some of them, including brain cells, are rarely replaced. Others are constantly replaced, as existing cells multiply to make new ones. However, each cell can only multiply a certain number of times before it dies. As more cells are lost or damaged, you start to show signs of ageing. For example, the fewer skin cells you have, the thinner your skin becomes.

What damages your cells?

Harmful molecules are continually bombarding your body. The worst offenders are glucose (a type of sugar), and free radicals, by-products of energy production. Both can damage the proteins, fats and DNA that make up your cells. When you are young, your body is able to repair most of this damage. But as you get older, the repair process is less efficient. Some researchers think that boosting our natural defences against these chemical onslaughts may lessen the effects of ageing.

How does a cell know how old it is?

Every time a cell multiplies to make two new cells, special zones at the ends of its chromosomes, called telomeres, become shorter. Once the telomeres reach a certain length, the cell stops dividing and eventually dies. The only cells to escape this fate are those that divide to make eggs and sperm. In these cells, a substance called telomerase builds the telomeres up again, so they remain the same length.

Can you prevent ageing?

A healthy lifestyle can help you feel younger and fitter for longer. Even people in their 90s can improve their muscle strength through regular exercise. Most research on ageing aims to improve our health and quality of life as we grow old, not make us live forever. Scientists are looking for ways to avoid, or even repair, the damage that causes ageing.

Can hormones slow ageing?

Hormones are your body's chemical messengers. One, called growth hormone (GH), controls bone growth and protein production. GH seems to play a crucial role in ageing: you stop making it somewhere between the ages of 60 and 90. Replacement GH may one day be used to counter some effects of old age, just as some women today use hormone replacement therapy (HRT).

Why don't we live forever?

Your life is not programmed to end, you simply wear out. But why don't your genes equip your body to live forever? One answer to this may lie in the past: our ancestors lived short, dangerous lives. They had children and passed on their genes while they were still young and fit. So, any genes that countered the effects of ageing (for example, those enabling better repair of the damage caused by free radicals) were not favoured by natural selection.

What is the cost of passing on genes?

To pass on our genes in a near-perfect condition to the next generation, our bodies must constantly repair any damage to the cells that make our eggs or sperm. This takes energy, leaving fewer resources for the rest of the body. One theory says that the rest of the body's cells are not as meticulously maintained, resulting in ageing.

Do you have genes for a long life?

In 1998, Japanese researchers found a 'long-life' version of a gene that is present in most people aged 100 or over. Scientists are also looking at other animals, particularly the nematode worm, to try and find genes

that affect life span. One version of a gene found in the nematode worm seems to double the worm's life span. Such genes probably help the body resist or repair cell damage more efficiently.

What goes on in a teenager's brain?

Moody? Risk-taking? Scientists are beginning to understand better the remarkable changes that go on in the teenage brain. Previously it was thought that your brain went through most of its development by the age of two. In fact, the brain undergoes many changes during adolescence. For example, as teens mature, their ability to recognise emotions improves. Brain imaging has shown they begin to use different regions of their brains, including areas linked with fear and 'gut' reactions and parts linked with more reasoned perception, to make these decisions.

What happens when the brain's function declines?

Some of us will develop diseases of the brain that affect our memory,

and how we understand and communicate. Alzheimer's disease is the most common form of dementia. Certain proteins have been found to damage brain cells. One type of protein forms 'plaques' which impair brain cells' function, causing them to die. A different type of protein forms 'tangles' which change the structure of brain cells. We also know that certain chemicals in the brain which transmit messages between neurons become depleted. Most forms of dementia cannot be cured, but research is continuing to identify treatments, including the development of drugs to help alleviate some of the symptoms.

⇨ The above information is reprinted with kind permission from the Science Museum. Please visit www.sciencemuseum.org.uk for further information on this and other subjects.

The number of centenarians in the UK has nearly quadrupled since 1981, from 2,600 to over 12,000 in 2010

Almost 1 in 5 of the UK's total population are of state pension age

There are now more people in the UK aged 60 and above ... than there are under 18

There are an estimated 575 - 810,000 lesbian, gay or bisexual people over state pension age in the UK

Over 2 million people over 75 live alone; 1.5 million of these are women

Each year, about 650,000 people turn 65

Source: Age UK. Later Life in the United Kingdom. October 2012, Age UK group © Age UK Group

Are you ready?
What you need to know about ageing

Our world is changing.

⇨ The number of people today aged 60 and over has doubled since 1980.

⇨ The number of people aged 80 years will almost quadruple to 395 million between now and 2050.

⇨ Within the next five years, the number of adults aged 65 and over will outnumber children under the age of five.

⇨ By 2050, these older adults will outnumber all children under the age of 14.

⇨ The majority of older people live in low- or middle-income countries. By 2050, this number will have increased to 80%.

⇨ In the 21st century, health is determined by and contributes to broad social trends. Economies are globalising, more and more people live and work in cities, family patterns are changing and technology is evolving rapidly. One of the biggest social transformations is population ageing. Soon, the world will have more older people than children and more people of very old age than ever before.

1. The world will have more people who live to see their 80s or 90s than ever before

The number of people aged 80 years or older, for example, will have almost quadrupled to 395 million between 2000 and 2050. There is no historical precedent for a majority of middle-aged and older adults having living parents, as is already the case today. More children will know their grandparents and even their great-grandparents, especially their great-grandmothers. On average, women live six to eight years longer than men.

2. The past century has seen remarkable improvements in life expectancy

In 1910, the life expectancy for a Chilean female was 33 years; today, a mere century later, it is 82 years. This represents a remarkable gain of almost 50 years of life in one century, and is largely due to improvements in public health.

3. Soon, the world will have more older people than children

Within the next five years, for the first time in human history, the number of adults aged 65 and over will outnumber children under the age of five. By 2050, these older adults will outnumber children under the age of 14.

4. The world population is rapidly ageing

Between 2000 and 2050, the proportion of the world's population over 60 years will double from about 11% to 22%. The absolute number of people aged 60 years and over is expected to increase from 605 million to two billion over the same period.

5. Low- and middle-income countries will experience the most rapid and dramatic demographic change

For example, it took more than 100 years for the share of France's population aged 65 or older to double from seven to 14%. In contrast, it will take countries like Brazil and China less than 25 years to reach the same growth.

Determinants of healthy ageing

1. Healthy ageing is linked to health in earlier stages of life

Undernutrition in the womb, for example, may increase the risk of disease in adult life, such as circulatory diseases and diabetes. Respiratory infections in childhood may increase the risk of chronic bronchitis in adult life. Obese, or overweight, adolescents run the risk

of developing chronic diseases, such as diabetes, circulatory disease, cancer, respiratory and musculo-skeletal disorders, in adult life.

2. Yet, how well we age depends on many factors

The functional capacity of an individual's biological system increases during the first years of life, reaches its peak in early adulthood and naturally declines thereafter. The rate of decline is determined, at least in part, by our behaviours and exposures across the whole life course. These include what we eat, how physically active we are and our exposure to health risks such as those caused by smoking, harmful consumption of alcohol, or exposure to toxic substances.

Demographic changes are accompanied by new challenges

1. Even in poor countries, most older people die of noncommunicable diseases

Even in poor countries, most older people die of noncommunicable diseases such as heart disease, cancer and diabetes, rather than from infectious and parasitic diseases. In addition, older people often have several health problems at the same time, such as diabetes and heart disease.

2. The number of people living with disability is increasing due to population ageing and because of the greater risk of chronic health problems in older age

For example, about 65% of all people who are visually impaired are aged 50 and older, with this age group comprising about 20% of the world's population. With an increasing elderly population in many countries, more people will be at risk of age-related visual impairment.

3. Globally, many older people are at risk of maltreatment

Around 4-6% of older people in developed countries have experienced some form of maltreatment at home. Abusive acts in institutions include physically restraining patients, depriving them of dignity (by for instance leaving them in soiled clothes) and intentionally providing insufficient care (such as allowing them to develop pressure sores). The maltreatment of older people can lead to serious physical injuries and long-term psychological consequences.

4. The need for long-term care is rising

The number of older people who are no longer able to look after themselves in developing countries is forecast to quadruple by 2050. Many of the very old lose their ability to live independently because of limited mobility, frailty or other physical or mental health problems. Many require some form of long-term care, which can include home nursing, community care and assisted living, residential care and long stays in hospitals.

5. Worldwide, there will be a dramatic increase in the number of people with dementias such as Alzheimer's disease, as people live longer

The risk of dementia rises sharply with age with an estimated 25-30% of people aged 85 or older having some degree of cognitive decline. Older people with dementia in low- and middle-income countries generally do not have access to the affordable long-term care their condition may warrant. Often their families do not have publicly funded support to help with care at home.

6. In emergency situations, older people can be especially vulnerable

When communities are displaced by natural disasters or armed conflict, older people may be unable to flee or travel long distances and may be left behind. Yet, in many situations they can also be a valuable resource for their communities as well as for the humanitarian aid process when they are involved as community leaders.

Fighting stereotypes

We all generally value and respect the older people we love or know well. But our attitudes to other older people within the broader community can be different. In many traditional societies, older people are respected as 'elders'. However, in other societies, older women and men may be less respected. The marginalisation can be structural, for example enforced retirement ages, or informal, such as older people being viewed as less energetic and less valuable to a potential employer. These attitudes are examples of 'ageism' – the stereotyping of, and discrimination against, individuals or groups because of their age. Ageist attitudes can portray older people as frail, 'past their sell-by date', unable to work, physically weak, mentally slow, disabled or helpless. Ageism serves as a social divider between young and old.

These stereotypes can prevent older men and women from fully participating in social, political, economic, cultural, spiritual, civic and other activities. Younger people may also influence these decisions in the attitudes they convey to older people, or even by building barriers to their participation.

We can escape this vicious cycle by breaking down stereotypes and change our attitudes about older people. Here are a few examples.

Stereotype 1: Older people are 'past their sell-by date'

While older workers are often presumed to be less productive than younger workers and studies show slight declines in information processing and attention with age, most individuals maintain mental competence and learning abilities well into older age. They also have the advantage of possessing experience and institutional memory. Deterioration in physical abilities may be much less than presumed. On 16 October 2011, British national Fauja Singh became the first 100-year-old to complete a marathon by running the Toronto Waterfront Marathon in Canada.

Stereotype 2: Older people are helpless

The fact that older people are particularly vulnerable in emergencies does not mean that older people in general are helpless. After the 2007 Cyclone Sidr in Bangladesh, older people's committees took an active role, disseminating early warning messages to people and families most at risk, identifying those who were worst hit, compiling beneficiary lists and notifying them when and where to receive relief goods. After the 2011 earthquake and Tsunami in Japan, older people and retirees came forward to volunteer at the nuclear disaster sites, saying they were not afraid of becoming contaminated with radiation. Advanced in years, they were less worried about the long-term impacts of the exposure.

Stereotype 3: Older people will eventually become senile

Occasional memory lapses are common at any age. And although the risk of developing dementia symptoms rises steeply with age in people over 60, possible signs of dementia (a loss of intellectual abilities), such as uncertainty about how to perform simple tasks, difficulty in completing sentences and confusion about the month or season, are not normal signs of ageing. Most older people are able to manage their financial affairs and their day-to-day lives. They can give informed consent for treatment or medical interventions they may need. In fact, some types of our memory stay the same or even continue to improve with age, as for example our semantic memory, which is the ability to recall concepts and general facts that are not related to specific experiences.

Stereotype 4: Older women have less value than younger women

People often equate women's worth with beauty, youth and the ability to have children. The role older women play in their families and communities, caring for their partners, parents, children and grandchildren is often overlooked. In most countries, women tend to be the family caregivers. Many take care of more than one generation. These women are often themselves at advanced ages. For example, in sub-Saharan Africa, 20% of rural women aged 60 and older are the main carers for their grandchildren.

Stereotype 5: Older people don't deserve health care

Treatable conditions and illnesses in older people are often overlooked or dismissed as being a 'normal part of ageing'. Age does not necessarily cause pain, and only extreme old age is associated with limitation of bodily function. The right to the best possible health does not diminish as we age: it is mainly society that sets age limits for access to complex treatments or proper rehabilitation and secondary prevention of disease and disability.

It is not age that limits the health and participation of older people. Rather, it is individual and societal misconceptions, discrimination and abuse that prevent active and dignified ageing.

29 May 2012

⇨ The above information is reprinted with kind permission from Dementia Today. Please visit www.dementiatoday.com.

Talkin' 'bout my generation

A look at young people's perceptions and opinions of age.

Introduction

What do young people think about age, ageing and the older generations? Do they believe that they are victims of discrimination? How do they feel about getting older? What do they think older generations can offer them and how do they view people of other ages?

In August 2010, London Youth ran a series of workshops with diverse groups of young people aged between 13 and 24 to enable them to explore some of these issues. Delivered in a fun and interactive way by a team of young trainers, the workshops stimulated discussion and challenged young people to look at their own perceptions of age.

Discrimination and stereotypes

The workshops began by examining the participants' views on discrimination and stereotyping. We asked the young people to draw and describe a stereotypical middle-aged person and an old person. There weren't many surprises here: young people classified the middle-aged character as stressed out and over-worked, and the older person as very grumpy, weak and unkempt with 'one foot in the grave'. We then asked them to draw and describe how they thought people of these generations saw them and what stereotypes and perceptions existed about young people. Interestingly, they all chose to represent the young person as a hoodie-wearing, knife-wielding label obsessive. It was unanimous that this was how they believed everyone, from people just a few years older than themselves up to old age pensioners, saw them.

The media

The amount of negative terminology surrounding young people stood out immediately and it was apparent that young people were very used to hearing themselves portrayed in a negative light and were almost resigned to this fact. The groups were savvy about the role of the media and were keenly aware of what sells newspapers, but explained their view that this prejudice against young people was causing a rift in society.

'It's the media that categorises people and we (the UK public) just follow what they say.'

They highlighted the lack of stories about young people who were doing well for themselves – the ones starting businesses, winning awards and volunteering. However, the focus was always on the ones causing trouble.

Age discrimination

To gain more of a sense of how age discrimination had impacted upon their lives the groups were asked to role play situations when they had felt they had been discriminated against because of their age. A young person spoke of going to see his local councillor to try to get more politically involved in his local community. He was told by the councillor to 'come back when he had lived his life', instantly denigrating his knowledge and experiences.

Another member of the group, a law student, told of her experiences on jury service where she felt her opinions were completely ignored due to her being 20 years younger than the others on the jury. Her suspicions were confirmed when she was told by a fellow juror that she was only young and so 'what did she know?'

The workplace

One of the key areas in which young people felt discriminated against was the workplace. Young people in each of the groups felt that they were overlooked when it came to meetings or opportunities and often felt patronised by older colleagues. People felt that complaining in these situations – which they said occurred frequently – would be difficult, as it was often just a look or the way that something was said. They were keenly aware of the importance of looking right and fitting in with older colleagues, although there was a sense that it was the young people who were forced to adapt rather than vice versa. Some of the group also felt they were overlooked at interviews and that jobs, opportunities and promotions always seemed to go to older (although not always more experienced) candidates.

Cultural issues

There were cultural difficulties too, and for those in the second generation from African or Asian backgrounds felt that age discrimination was deeply

'The media perception of young people is that there are some good ones out there but the majority are up to no good. They're not the same as they were 20, 30, 40 years ago. There's a slight negative feeling about the young people we have today. What I see and what I hear never seems to be good, you don't hear about the brilliant things that young people do.'

entrenched. Members of the group from Nigerian backgrounds spoke about the difficulties of coming from a culture that puts a significant weight on age. Being second generation with Nigerian parents often means a clash of views, with the younger generation trying to get across the message that in Britain it's about ability and not age. Many also linked age discrimination to cultural discrimination, with older people (and the media) finding it more acceptable to publically criticise a young person's youth than their cultural or racial background, although this would be implied in the criticism.

Getting older

The majority of the group confessed that they didn't spend any time considering getting older – and that even if they did it was just the next few years ahead of them. They had felt certain milestones pass – most mentioned the end of free travel as a real marker of not being a child anymore – but their time frame was very limited.

The general feeling towards getting older within the group was one of both excitement and fear. It was exciting to consider what it would be like to grow up on Facebook or other social networking platforms,

Perceptions of age

Term	Age range
Baby	0-2
Infants	3-6
Child	7-10
Young teen	10-13
Teenager	13-18/19
Young adult	18/19-25
Adult	26-35
Mature adult	36-45
Middle age	45/50-60
Senior citizen/OAP	60-70
Elderly	70+

'I really felt that age was in fact an issue as I was the youngest person there. It became like a barrier for me as the older jury members didn't value my opinion at all, which I believe was a result of my age. At times I felt belittled, which, as a law student, I did not appreciate!'

watching the stories of their lives unfold for everyone to see. The fear seemed to stem from the amount of responsibilities linked to getting older: jobs, marriage, mortgages and having families. Although most aspired to achieve these things in their lives they were also worried about losing the feeling of freedom they had loved in their early teens.

'There's so much responsibility about getting older; money, work, babies, husbands, houses and mortgages. It sounds really stressful. I'd rather just be carefree and not have to worry about all of that.'

Another fear was being in a position when they were meant to know all of the answers. They felt that, as young people, it was okay to make mistakes and there was less pressure to get things right.

What did young people want from older people?

Young people could clearly see the benefit of working with older people, in particular those who were the generation or two above them. In fact, most of them seemed to really want it. They regarded the older generations as having the answers, being able to tell them how to get where they want to go and give them support on the journey. The young people felt that although they knew what they wanted, they needed to break some sort of 'glass ceiling' to get there. Many of the group were the first generation to go to university in their family and felt that although their parents want them to make a success of themselves, they weren't often in a position to advise them on how to get there.

They also wanted to be understood better and to be judged on merit rather than age, especially in the working environment. Maybe older people could take time to consider themselves when they were the same age?

'I look at adults like they were never ever young. It feels to me that they were always old because they look at young people as though they were never like, they were never this age, they were always the way they are. And it really does frustrate me because in order for us to get where older people are, we're going to need the help of adults who have been there before.'

When asked about the importance of specific intergenerational projects, most saw the benefit but were unclear as to what these would look like. They did agree that it would be important that people were brought together on common ground and with a common goal. For projects to genuinely make a difference on both sides all participants would need to be on an even playing field with everyone working together for mutual benefit.

August 2010

⇨ The above information is from London Youth, and is reprinted with permission. Please visit www.londonyouth.org.uk for further information on this and other subjects.

© London Youth

UK performs poorly on experience of ageing

Information from Mature Times.

The experience of ageing in the UK is poor compared to other EU countries, with older people in this country the loneliest, poorest and the most concerned about age discrimination, according to a major report by older people's charity, WRVS.

The research, which focuses on a range of indicators, including health, wealth and levels of loneliness in four countries (the UK, Germany, the Netherlands and Sweden), graded the UK third in its overall performance.

Loneliness and lacking somebody to confide in are a particular problem in the UK, the report concludes. Older people in the UK have the highest rates of loneliness and they feel – more than older people in the other three countries – that they do not socialise as much as other people their age. One reason for this may be long-term underinvestment by local authorities in services that reduce isolation and loneliness.

FUNNY, THAT THE MORE EFFORT WE MAKE, THE BETTER WE FEEL!

In terms of the overall health of over-65's, the UK performs relatively poorly. It has the highest prevalence of life-limiting illness among older people and the lowest score for 'feeling active and vigorous'. This may reflect particularly unhealthy lifestyles in the UK, with higher rates of alcohol consumption and obesity than in the other three countries. In Sweden, whose older people are the healthiest of the four countries, public policy focuses on improving people's health earlier on in life to ensure that they have a healthier old age.

On average, UK pensioners have the lowest net income of the four countries and are most likely to have had to draw on savings or economise on their expenditure in the last three years. Older people in the UK also have the lowest perception of their own living standards.

Out of the four countries, Britain's over 65s are at the highest risk of poverty, with a fifth of pensioners at risk of poverty in 2010, compared to only six per cent of pensioners at risk of poverty in the Netherlands. This is particularly worrying, as the report finds that there is a clear correlation between income and health and income and social participation amongst older people, with poorer older people demonstrating worse health and lower levels of social participation.

The UK ranks the lowest on the age discrimination theme, while Sweden performs particularly well, with a mean score that was higher by several points. This study found that:

⇨ On average people surveyed in the UK believe that old age starts at age 59, compared to an average of 61.9 in Germany, 62.2 in Sweden and 62.9 in the Netherlands

⇨ Older people in the UK feel more negative towards young people in their 20s than older people in Germany, Sweden and the Netherlands

⇨ Older people in the UK more frequently feel that they have been shown a lack of respect because of their age than older people in the other three countries

⇨ When examined by gender, it was found that older women in the UK were more concerned about age discrimination than older men

⇨ People in the UK are also particularly concerned, in comparison to the other three countries, that there is too much age segregation in society and that there are not enough opportunities for older and younger people to work together and socialise.

David McCullough, chief executive, WRVS, comments:

'This research highlights the sad truth about growing old in Britain today and should act as a wake up call. The treatment of older people in this country needs to be addressed and we must learn from our EU partners. They have proved that it is possible to tackle some of these issues by taking advantage of volunteers to provide older people with more social contact and better links to their communities. This in turn will have a knock on beneficial impact on their health.'

'From WRVS' own experience working with older people, we know that increased social interaction and more socialising between generations are hugely beneficial in combating not only loneliness, but also health problems. This, in turn, can keep people happier, healthier and out of hospital and in their homes for longer. But we need to reach more people and to do this we need to double our volunteer workforce.'

'WRVS, with the Campaign to End Loneliness, is developing a toolkit that will help local commissioners to identify and tackle loneliness in their areas.'

The report makes a number of recommendations, including:

The Netherlands and Sweden have high rates of volunteering. There is huge potential to harness the social and political resources of the retiring baby boomer generation in the UK to provide peer support to older people and increase the opportunities for social participation locally.

The Government should produce annual reports on Britain's older population, including detailed indicators that cut across income, health and social issues and benchmarking progress against other EU countries.

The UK needs to tackle our particularly high perceptions of age discrimination.

The UK should explore what more can be done to encourage intergenerational mingling. This should include consideration of social environments, volunteering and the workplace.

25 May 2012

⇨ The above information is reprinted with kind permission from Mature Times. Please visit www. maturetimes.co.uk for further information on this and other subjects.

Older people are happier in Brazil and South Africa

Information from Politics.co.uk.

Contrary to belief, older people in South Africa and Brazil become happier as they age. New research suggests that, with the right policies in place, a developing country can significantly improve the well-being of its older citizens.

The average levels of well-being experienced by older people in South Africa and Brazil improved between 2002 and 2008, due to a combination of economic growth and enlightened social policies, according to a study from the New Dynamics of Ageing Programme, a unique collaboration between five UK Research Councils.

'Our work contradicts many of the assumptions people have about the fate of older people in developing countries,' said Professor Armando Barrientos, Research Director at Manchester University's Brooks World Poverty Institute. 'It's often assumed that people will become poorer and increasingly unhappy with life as they become old, but in South Africa and Brazil the opposite seems to have happened,' he said.

The research explored the factors that influence well-being among the elderly populations of the two countries. Brazil and South Africa were chosen because of their far-reaching social policies. 'They are leading countries in their respective regions, with innovative social policies addressing poverty and vulnerability, such as child and disability benefits, low interest loans for the elderly and non-contributory pension schemes,' explained Professor Barrientos.

This large study included a survey of around 1,000 households. When the new data was compared with data collected in 2002, it suggested well-being had improved and that the majority of older people in the two countries felt satisfied or very satisfied with their lives. A majority of older people in each country also said they were satisfied with their relationships with other family members and with the respect they received from others.

The improvement in well-being was strongly influenced by economic performance and labour market conditions, but social policy also played a significant role. For low-income families, the pension income received by elderly people was essential to both their objective standard of living and their feeling that life was getting better.

'The research has important lessons for policymakers in the developing world,' says Professor Barrientos. 'Populations in the developing world are growing much faster than they did in the countries that we now consider as developed,' he said. 'That means governments in these nations have far less time to deal with the challenge of an ageing population, and they cannot just copy the policies used in developed countries.'

There are lessons for the developed world too, he believes. 'Many countries in the developed world have been moving towards the idea that the state should provide only a minimal pension,' he said. 'But our research suggests governments might want to think more carefully about the wider social value of decent state pension provision.'

3 October 2011

⇨ The above information is from politics.co.uk. Please visit www.politics.co.uk for further information on this and other subjects.

Lesbian, gay and bisexual people in later life

Summary and key findings from Stonewall.

Stonewall asked YouGov to survey a sample of 1,050 heterosexual and 1,036 lesbian, gay and bisexual people over the age of 55 across Britain. The survey asked about their experiences and expectations of getting older and examined their personal support structures, family connections and living arrangements. It also asked about how they feel about getting older, the help they expect to need, and what they would like to be available from health and social care services.

Getting older can be much more complex for lesbian, gay and bisexual people than heterosexual people, as they are more likely to face the prospect either alone or without as much personal support as their heterosexual counterparts.

'My family rejected me a long time ago hence no contact or support – no children and my partner of 43 years died from cancer as soon as we retired'
Neil, 67, North West

Lesbian, gay and bisexual people over 55 are:

⇨ More likely to be single. Gay and bisexual men are almost three times more likely to be single than heterosexual men, 40 per cent compared to 15 per cent.

⇨ More likely to live alone. 41 per cent of lesbian, gay and bisexual people live alone compared to 28 per cent of heterosexual people.

⇨ Less likely to have children. Just over a quarter of gay and bisexual men and half of lesbian and bisexual women have children compared to almost nine in ten heterosexual men and women.

⇨ Less likely to see biological family members on a regular basis. Less than a quarter of lesbian, gay and bisexual people see their biological family members at least once a week compared to more than half of heterosexual people.

Lesbian, gay and bisexual people share many worries about ageing with their heterosexual peers but are consistently more anxious across a range of issues including future care needs, independence and mobility, health including mental health and housing. Half feel that their sexual orientation has, or will have, a negative effect on getting older.

A healthy lifestyle is important and while the smoking trends of older lesbian, gay and bisexual people broadly follow those of heterosexual people, there are other notable differences.

Older lesbian, gay and bisexual people:

⇨ Drink alcohol more often. 45 per cent drink alcohol at least 'three or four days' a week compared to just 31 per cent of heterosexual people.

⇨ Are more likely to take drugs. One in 11 have taken drugs within the last year compared to one in 50 heterosexual people.

⇨ Are more likely to have a history of mental ill health and have more concerns about their mental health in the future.

⇨ Lesbian and bisexual women are more likely to have ever been diagnosed with depression and anxiety – two in five have been diagnosed with depression, one in three with anxiety.

⇨ Gay and bisexual men are twice as likely to have ever been diagnosed with depression and anxiety than heterosexual men.

⇨ 49 per cent of lesbian, gay and bisexual people worry about their mental health compared to 37 per cent of heterosexual people.

With diminished support networks in comparison to their heterosexual peers, more lesbian, gay and bisexual people expect they will need to rely on formal support services as they get older. Lesbian, gay and bisexual people are nearly twice as likely as their heterosexual peers to expect to rely on a range of external services, including GPs, health and social care services and paid help.

However, at the same time, lesbian, gay and bisexual people feel that providers of services won't be able to understand and meet their needs.

⇨ Three in five are not confident that social care and support services, like paid carers, or housing services would be able to understand and meet their needs.

⇨ More than two in five are not confident that mental health services would be able to understand and meet their needs.

⇨ One in six are not confident that their GP and other health services would be able to understand and meet their needs.

As a result nearly half would be uncomfortable 'being out' to care home staff, a third would be uncomfortable 'being out' to a housing provider, hospital staff or a paid carer, and approximately one in five wouldn't feel comfortable disclosing their sexual orientation to their GP.

Significant numbers of disabled lesbian, gay and bisexual people also report that they have not accessed the health, mental health and social care services in the last year that they felt they needed.

The cumulative experience and concerns of older lesbian, gay and bisexual people leave them specifically concerned about the prospect either of living alone without support or having to enter care homes which will not meet their needs.

⇨ The above information is reprinted with kind permission from Stonewall. Please visit www.stonewall.org.uk for further information on this and other subjects.

Implementing a ban on age discrimination in the NHS – making effective, appropriate decisions

Executive summary.

From 1 October 2012, the Government will fully implement the ban on age discrimination enshrined in the Equality Act 2010, giving protection against age discrimination in services, clubs and associations and in the exercise of public functions. This is one of the last parts of the Act to come into force in England, Wales and Scotland.

This briefing gives a short overview of the ban on age discrimination. It is specifically aimed at those who plan, commission or provide NHS services, whether in the NHS, voluntary or private sectors.

From 1 October 2012, it will be unlawful for service providers and commissioners to discriminate, victimise or harass a person because of age. A person will be protected when requesting, and during the course of being provided with, goods, facilities and services. If a member of the public aged 18 or over believes that they have been treated less favourably because of age,

they will be able to take organisations or individuals to court – and may be awarded compensation. A case could be taken against health organisations (such as hospitals or commissioning bodies), individual clinicians (e.g. consultants, GPs or allied health professionals) or others working in the health sector (such as managers).

Age can play a part when professionals make decisions about the care and treatment that patients receive and in some cases this will be wholly appropriate. What is not acceptable practice, and could also be viewed as unlawful by the courts, is where a professional acts or makes a decision based on a stereotypical view of age and how that individual lives their life. Age must not be used as a proxy for the proper assessment of individual need.

Age discrimination is unfairly treating people differently because of their age. The ban is only intended to prevent harmful uses of age. Positive use of age in providing, commissioning and planning services will be able to continue. The Act does not prevent differential treatment where this is objectively justified. Policy makers, commissioners, providers and individuals working in health and social care should continue to take into account someone's chronological age when it is right and beneficial to do so.

28 September 2012

⇨ The above information is reprinted with kind permission from The Department of Health. Please visit www.wp.dh.gov.uk for further information.

What is ageism?

Ageism is discrimination or unfair treatment based on a person's age. It can impact on someone's confidence, job prospects, financial situation and quality of life. It can also include the way that older people are represented in the media, which can have a wider impact on the public's attitudes.

It's important that ageism, often called age discrimination, is addressed to ensure that nobody loses out because of their age.

Perhaps you have been in a situation where you have been discriminated against due to your age. You may be fully aware that you have been subject to ageism, but sometimes it's not so obvious.

Although ageism is often seen as a workplace issue, you may face it when you're out shopping, at the doctor's surgery, or even when ordering products and services over the phone.

Older people may experience...

⇨ Losing a job because of their age.

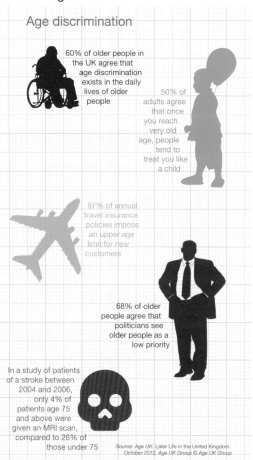

Age discrimination

60% of older people in the UK agree that age discrimination exists in the daily lives of older people

50% of adults agree that once you reach very old age, people tend to treat you like a child

97% of annual travel insurance policies impose an upper age limit for new customers

68% of older people agree that politicians see older people as a low priority

In a study of patients of a stroke between 2004 and 2006, only 4% of patients age 75 and above were given an MRI scan, compared to 26% of those under 75

Source: Age UK. Later Life in the United Kingdom. October 2012, Age UK Group © Age UK Group

⇨ Being refused interest-free credit, a new credit card, car insurance or travel insurance because of their age.

⇨ Receiving a lower quality of service in a shop or restaurant because of the organisation's attitude to older people.

⇨ Not being eligible for benefits such as Disability Living Allowance due to age limits.

⇨ Being refused a referral from a doctor to a consultant because you are 'too old'.

⇨ Being refused membership to a club or trade association because of your age.

All of these situations are examples of ageism. You are protected against some of these situations by law, but not all of them.

Under the Equality Act, you are protected from ageism in employment, training and education, and also in membership of clubs and associations. Unfortunately, there is no protection in some areas, including housing, as yet. From 1 October 2012, you will have increased protection when you are receiving products and services, to ensure you aren't treated unfairly.

Ageism in recruitment

If an employer turns you down for a job because you are too old or too young, this is ageism in recruitment and it is unlawful. Discrimination laws protect you when you apply for a job as well as while you are working.

Does this apply to all ages?

Previously, an employer could refuse to consider candidates for jobs if they were over 65 (or the firm's normal retirement age). Since the default retirement age was abolished under the Equality Act 2010 and started being phased out in April 2011, this can no longer be used as a justifiable reason.

What about job adverts?

Employers can't include age limits in job adverts, and should avoid using words which could suggest they are looking for applicants from a particular age group – for example, by using terms such as 'ten years' experience', 'enthusiastic young people' or ' recent graduates'. They can ask for your date of birth – for example, to check you are over 18 if necessary, or to see whether they are attracting a wide range of candidates – but they should keep this separate from the application and mustn't use it as a deciding factor in whether to give you the job.

Agency workers

Agency workers now have the same rights as permanent employees. Agencies mustn't discriminate against you because of your age. For example, they can't deny you access to their services or to particular job placements based on your age.

How do you prove discrimination in recruitment?

Ageism during the recruitment process can be difficult to prove, as the employer is unlikely to make their reasons obvious. If you think an employer discriminated against you when you applied for a job, there is a questionnaire that you can use to get information from them to decide whether to bring a claim against them. The questionnaire can also help you to gather evidence if you decide to go ahead. You can download it from the Home Office website.

What about positive action?

Positive action is now lawful in certain situations, to help to ensure that groups of people with protected characteristics are not disadvantaged. For example, an employer may in some circumstances be able to justify their selection of one candidate over another who is equally well suited to the job because they are older or female, and the workplace currently has a lack of older or female employees. However, there are strict guidelines that employers must follow. Positive action can also be used in providing access to education and training facilities.

Ageism in the workplace

Age discrimination at work is unlawful. You should not be treated any differently to your colleagues because of your age, unless your employer can objectively justify it. For instance, fire fighters and airline pilots can be made to retire at 65 on the grounds of health and safety.

You are protected from age discrimination, or ageism, in all aspects of your employment, including:

⇨ recruitment

⇨ employment terms and conditions

⇨ promotions and transfers

⇨ training

⇨ dismissals.

For example, your employer cannot exclude you from a training course that younger employees are going on because you're older, and they cannot pass you over for a promotion you would otherwise have been given, on the grounds of your age.

⇨ The above information is reprinted with kind permission from Age UK. Please visit www.ageuk.org.uk for further information.

Ten priority actions to maximise the opportunity of ageing populations

An extract from the United Nations Population Fund and HelpAge International report Ageing in the Twenty-First Century: A Celebration and a Challenge.

1. Recognise the inevitability of population ageing and the need to adequately prepare all stakeholders (governments, civil society, private sector, communities, and families) for the growing numbers of older persons. This should be done by enhancing understanding, strengthening national and local capacities, and developing the political, economic and social reforms needed to adapt societies to an ageing world.

2. Ensure that all older persons can live with dignity and security, enjoying access to essential health and social services and a minimum income through the implementation of national social protection floors and other social investments that extend the autonomy and independence of older people, prevent impoverishment in old age and contribute to a more healthy ageing. These actions should be based on a long-term vision, and supported by a strong political commitment and a secured budget that prevents negative impacts in time of crisis or governmental changes.

3. Support communities and families to develop support systems which ensure that frail older persons receive the long-term care they need and promote active and healthy ageing at the local level to facilitate ageing in place.

4. Invest in young people today by promoting healthy habits, and ensuring education and employment opportunities, access to health services, and social security coverage for all workers as the best investment to improve the lives of future generations of older persons. Flexible employment, life-long learning and retraining opportunities should be promoted to facilitate the integration in the labour market of current generations of older persons.

5. Support international and national efforts to develop comparative research on ageing, and ensure that gender and culture-sensitive data and evidence from this research are available to inform policy making.

6. Mainstream ageing into all gender policies and gender into ageing policies, taking into account the specific requirements of older women and men.

7. Ensure inclusion of ageing and the needs of older persons in all national development policies and programmes.

8. Ensure inclusion of ageing and the needs of older persons in national humanitarian response, climate change mitigation and adaptation plans, and disaster management and preparedness programmes.

9. Ensure that ageing issues are adequately reflected in the post-2015 development agenda, including through the development of specific goals and indicators.

10. Develop a new rights-based culture of ageing and a change of mindset and societal attitudes towards ageing and older persons, from welfare recipients to active, contributing members of society. This requires, among others, working towards the development of international human rights instruments and their translation into national laws and regulations and affirmative measures that challenge age discrimination and recognise older people as autonomous subjects.

⇨ This report was published by the United Nations Population Fund (UNFPA), New York, and HelpAge International, London. Please visit www.helpage.org for further information.

Does life begin again at retirement?

Information from Campbell Harrison.

There are numerous clichés about age; 40 is the 'top of the hill', 'life begins at 50' and of course the party animal 18-year-old to name a few. People look forward to certain milestones in their lives, and one milestone that the majority of people look forward to is the retirement age. Although this age keeps rising, people plan what they will do when they have retired and how they will be able to afford all of the things they want to do. Hopefully, most people will have undertaken a lot of retirement planning throughout the course of their life so they have enough money to live comfortably and do things they wouldn't usually do like go on an extended holiday or even volunteer full time. If a person has not started planning for how they will cope with retirement financially, they need to start thinking about it.

Many financial advisers recommend using a 'retirement calculator'. This will tell people when they can retire so they can start planning how many years they have to save money as part of their own pension plan. However, there is more to retirement than just living a comfortable life; retirement is for having fun and doing things you could never do before.

Many retirees who have worked all of their life may find that, after a few weeks rest, they begin to miss work. Many people enjoy having a routine and feeling like they are doing something worthwhile. The social aspects of volunteering are also good for retirees as they continue to make new friends and have a group of people to talk to every day. A person will only be able to volunteer if they have saved enough money throughout their life to not need a paying job after they retire. Volunteers often find that giving something back to the community, or working towards something they're passionate about, is a great way of keeping alert and healthy.

Other people who retire may want to spend a lot of money on a lifetime ambition, for example, on a road trip across the US with a friend or partner. This can cost thousands of pounds, but if a person has been thinking about it for some time and has saved up the money they need through their pension plan provider and through their own personal account, they will be able to afford to do whatever it is that they want to do.

For some people, life does begin at retirement as they are able to do what they want to do without the pressures of work. However, to be able to have this luxury, it is important that people plan for their retirement throughout their working life.

29 May 2012

⇨ The above information is reprinted with kind permission from retirement and investment planners Campbell Harrison. Please visit www.campbellharrison.co.uk for further information.

The dangers of our ageing population

More must be done to prepare this country as its people grow older.

We are not so much living in an age of crisis as facing a crisis of age. Its latest manifestation was the warning from the International Monetary Fund that demographic pressures will impose unexpectedly onerous financial burdens on industrialised countries. For Britain, the IMF calculated that on the 'not unreasonable' assumption that the entire cost would fall on taxpayers, the country's public debt would rise from 76 per cent of gross domestic product to as much as 135 per cent – or £750 billion at today's prices. This is clearly unsustainable and has not been planned for, not least because we have persistently underestimated the speed with which average lifespans are rising. As a result, government pension policies – which are difficult enough as it is to frame – tend to lag three years behind the demographic reality.

By any historical standard, the rapid ageing of the population represents a great economic and social transformation. There are more people over 65 than under 16.

In future, the numbers aged over 65 will be far greater than now, and whereas until fairly recently four people of working age supported every pensioner, that ratio is set to decline dramatically. It is a good thing that people live longer and do, by and large, stay healthy and fit well into old age. But the implications are enormous; and while the Government is addressing some of the issues that arise, there is none of the urgency that is needed. If nothing is done, age-related spending, particularly on health care and pensions, will start to increase very significantly from the mid-2020s, but tax revenues will not be growing to match.

To be fair, the Government is not oblivious to the dangers. As Steve Webb, the Minister for Pensions, explained in this newspaper on Monday, private sector pensions have had to adjust to the new realities, with most closing down final salary schemes. But more is needed. Management fees must be controlled because they erode the value of private pensions and discourage people from saving; and

without adequate savings, many will face a penurious old age with little state support to fall back on. In addition, public sector pensions must come into line with those in the private sector, to release more money for people to provide for themselves. It is hard to believe that the teachers' unions, among others, are still threatening to strike over pensions, despite being offered a generous deal. It will also be necessary automatically to link the state pension age to life expectancy and to publish regular actuarial calculations of where the dates might fall. This would reintroduce a small element of certainty into what is otherwise a very uncertain future.

12 April 2012

⇨ The above article originally appeared in *The Telegraph* and is reprinted with permission. Please visit www.telegraph. co.uk for further information.

Why our ageing population is an asset not a burden

Information from *The Huffington Post.*

The growing number of older people throughout Europe offers us an immense opportunity. Older people, after all, constitute an army within which there is knowledge, talent and ability. Many older people are already crucial to our businesses and services. But in some cases, especially in the more developed economies of the EU, outdated attitudes and practices around work and retirement have tended to marginalise older people and turn them, often prematurely, from being contributors to being recipients. The opposite to what is needed as countries strive to find the magic formula by which their flagging economies can be revitalized.

The point is that there is, regardless of many media portrayals of older people, no problem arising from ageing in itself. Rather there is a political challenge, the response to which must start with the question that asks 'how can we better harness longevity as an asset'?

At the new Age Research Centre within Coventry University we are exploring the answers to this question – poised to give sound advice as to how politicians and others can rise to the challenge. One of our objectives is to make the case, backed up by clear evidence, for a new appreciation of both the actual and potential contribution made by older people to our economic and social life.

But we recognise at the same time, the harsh reality that with older age comes both physical and cognitive decline. Regrettably, policy and practice frameworks, underpinned sometimes by ageist attitudes, may have served to hasten such decline because of their tendency to marginalise rather than facilitate the inclusion and engagement of older people. Such marginalisation we argue arises, in part, from attitudes that attribute a lesser value to older people who are not in paid work – regardless of their actual contributions. This especially affects older women. Small wonder that many older people are poorly motivated and have internalised negative views of themselves.

But even where there is marginalisation and some dependency it is essential to ensure that older people, as for adults of all ages, are afforded options and choices by which they can adopt and maintain lifestyles that are conducive to their better health and well-being. We must, therefore, endorse the World Health Organisation adage that affirms 'while years have been added to life; now we must add life to years'.

This means that we call for more flexibility in approaches to age at all its stages, by which we can begin to break away from the notion of progression along some kind of conveyor belt that would have us all pursue a clear path of education, work and then retirement. Greater flexibility means that, instead, we might enjoy different options across the life-course – to enable people to work full or part-time, to take time out (for caring responsibilities, etc.), for training and development or for career changes.

All in all, this points to a scenario where there are more older people who are active (and visible) in the workplace – as employees or employers. And if we can move towards frameworks that facilitate this, then there is the potential to harness the knowledge, talent and ability that many older people possess. There would be, furthermore, the benefit of older people's presence that will help to demolish some of the misconceptions and stereotypes. Older people, meanwhile, will increasingly look for 'employers of choice' who offer age-friendly working conditions.

To help employers think about their approach to older age, Coventry University is already working with ACAS (The Arbitration Conciliation and Advisory Service in the UK) to create an 'age audit' tool for use by employers. This will help them to gauge the extent to which they secure the engagement and respond to the needs and aspirations of their older workers. This audit will, we envisage, add to the evidence regarding the reliability and loyalty of older workers; this, in turn, possibly pointing to the need for employers to give extra consideration to their training and developmental needs.

More broadly with regard to the well-being of older people, we see a clear need for health services to place greater emphasis on prevention and to reconfigure service frameworks in ways that encourage us all to take more responsibility for our own health. Housing and communities, meanwhile, need to be increasingly designed with accessibility and usability in mind. And in all contexts there is the potential for assistive technologies to help meet the needs of people at work, at home or on the move.

What this means is that an ageing population is only a problem if workplaces and attitudes do not evolve in ways that facilitate the greater involvement and engagement of older people. This requires a recognition that older people are an important asset. And with regard to the prosperity and vitality of our future communities and workplaces, we ignore this asset at our peril.

26 July 2012

⇨ The above information is from *The Huffington Post* and is reproduced with permission from AOL (UK). Please visit www.huffingtonpost.co.uk for further information.

More than one in five British pensioners at risk of poverty

Information from Pensioners Campaign UK.

British pensioners are among Europe's poorest, with more than two million older people at risk of poverty, official figures reveal. The UK is ranked fourth out of 27 European countries in data from the Office for National Statistics, behind only Cyprus, Bulgaria and Spain.

'People are defined as being at risk of poverty if their disposable income is below 60 per cent of the UK median disposable income'

More than one in five (21.4 per cent) of older British people were classed as being at risk of poverty in 2010, 'significantly higher' than the EU average of 15.9 per cent, the ONS said. Charities said the figures should be a 'wake-up call' to the plight of millions of older people and called for a radical shake-up of the pension system.

'The Government must continue to work proactively on ways of getting money to older people'

Michelle Mitchell, of Age UK said: 'The Government must continue to work proactively on ways of getting money to older people in desperate need. Independent information and advice and face-to-face communication are key to improving the take-up of benefits.'

Ros Altmann, director of Saga, said: 'We have had a system of state pensions that has been systematically cut over the years, trying to offload responsibility on

to the private sector. It is another demonstration of why radical reform of our pension system is long overdue.'

The highest poverty rates among over-65s were found in Cyprus (45.2 per cent), Bulgaria (32.2 per cent) and Spain (21.7 per cent). The lowest were in Hungary (4.1 per cent), the Netherlands (5.9 per cent) and Luxembourg (5.9 per cent). Overall, 17.1 per cent of the total UK population, or 10.7 million people, were at risk of poverty in 2010, the ONS said. This was down from 19.0 per cent in 2005, but was still higher than the EU average of 16.4 per cent.

People are defined as being at risk of poverty if their disposable income is below 60 per cent of the UK median disposable income. The at-risk rate has declined as average disposable incomes fell after the credit crunch of 2008. This means some individuals whose incomes were just below the threshold in 2008 were no longer classified as being at risk of poverty in 2009, even if their incomes had not changed.

Britain had the 10th highest at risk of poverty rate among the 27 EU states in 2010. The highest rates were in Latvia (21.3 per cent), Romania (21.1 per cent) and Spain and Bulgaria (both 20.7 per cent).

The lowest rates were found in the Czech Republic (9 per cent), the Netherlands (10.3 per cent), Slovakia (12 per cent) and Austria (12.1 per cent).

⇨ The above information is reprinted with kind permission from Pensioners Campaign UK. Please visit www.pensionerscampaignuk. webspace.virginmedia.com for further information on this and other subjects.

Pensioners in work doubled since 1993

The number of older workers in the UK has almost doubled from 753,000 in 1993 to 1.4 million in 2011, according to official figures.

By Adam Jolley

Over the period, the number remained relatively flat until the year 2000, before rising more steeply to a peak of 1.45 million in 2010, data from the Office for National Statistics (ONS) shows.

An older worker is defined as someone working beyond state pension age (SPA) – the earliest age you can get your state pension.

The increase in older workers is being attributed to an ageing population and post-World War II baby-boomer generation, which is now reaching SPA.

Wanting to remain active in society and financial pressures could also be influencing the decision for more people to work longer.

A new retirement reality

Vince Smith-Hughes, retirement expert at Prudential, believes the figures reflect a permanent change.

Smith-Hughes said: 'There is a new retirement reality taking shape across the UK, as an increasing number of older workers make the decision to continue working past 65.

'More than ten per cent of people who had planned to retire this year are making alternative arrangements and putting off drawing their pension for the time being.

'This is driven in part by a desire to remain physically healthy and mentally active, but also to ensure they have sufficient funds to meet rising living costs and provide for a comfortable retirement.

'Those retiring at 65 will face an average of 19 years in retirement which makes the financial and social benefits of working for longer an even bigger draw.'

UK pensioners among poorest in EU

The figures come a week after ONS data showed pensioners in Britain are among the poorest in Europe.

More than a fifth – 21.4 per cent – of over-65s are at risk of poverty, compared with the EU average of 15.9 per cent.

This places the UK fourth on a list of pensioner poverty in the EU, behind only Cyprus, Bulgaria and Spain.

People are defined as at risk of poverty if their disposable income is 60 per cent or more below the national average.

Overall the UK has the tenth highest rate among the 27 EU member states – in 2010 17.1 per cent of the population were classed as at risk of poverty, equivalent to 10.7 million people.

Pensioner poverty

Mike Morrison, head of pension development at AXA Wealth, said: 'We know that the state pension in the UK is relatively low, but when put into a "league table" like this it looks even worse, particularly as there will be a lot of EU countries that we would expect to see below us.'

Morrison added: 'I must stress that this is "relative" poverty as opposed to "absolute" poverty and therefore will depend on the overall standard of living – the national average income – in the country concerned.

'Nonetheless, it doesn't make comfortable reading.'

13 June 2012

⇨ The above article was written by Adam Jolley, a writer for price comparison site Confused.com, and is reprinted with permission. Please visit www.confused.com for further information.

Pension gap:
a father's and son's tale

The father retired at 49. His son is 33 and has yet to start a pension.

Work longer than your dad, and retire on less. That is the Father's Day message from a slew of new data that highlights the growing gulf between the pensioners of today and the retirement prospects of the younger generation.

Straining under the weight of mortgage payments, credit card debts and student loans, pension saving is slipping down the list of priorities of today's young families. Yet the longer they put off retirement saving, the more the gap between the pensions they can expect and those enjoyed by their parents grows.

UK pensions have hit an all-time low, according to research from Scottish Widows, with only 46% of people saving enough for their retirement, five percentage points down on last year and a fall of eight percentage points from 2009. More than one in five, 22%, are putting aside nothing at all for later life.

While pension saving is falling, the amount people believe they need to be comfortable in retirement is actually rising, with £24,500 the average level of annual income people would feel comfortable living on at age 70, compared with £24,300 in 2011, according to the report.

But the reality is that low pension saving is leading to increasing numbers of people working longer. The number of people still in jobs after state pension age has almost doubled over the past decade, from 753,000 in 1993 to 1.4 million in 2011, according to new figures from the Office for National Statistics. These figures come just weeks after a report from insurer LV= predicted that more than six million people were on course to retire on less than the minimum wage.

Calum and John Laurie, both of West Lothian, are a perfect example of the way retirement expectations are in decline. Calum, a 57-year-old retired police officer who still consults for the force, has an index-linked pension of two thirds of his salary, which he has been receiving since age 49. John has no pension at all so far, even though at 33 he is just 16 years younger than the age at which his father retired. He expects to have to work until he is 69 at least, and will not receive any state pension until a year earlier.

Father and son's different experiences of finance reflect the changing face of our society. 'Things were so much simpler when I was a young man,' said Calum. 'Credit was so much harder to get and when I joined the police you were simply enrolled into the scheme with no opt out, so there was no question of not having a pension.'

Retirement planning is less straightforward for John, a father of two who runs his own outdoor fitness business. John has seen the credit binge of a decade ago catch up with him, and has little spare cash to pay into a pension. With credit cards, student debts and car finance loans compounded into a £23,000 second charge on top of his £130,000 mortgage, he is struggling to find the cash to contribute into a pension.

He has done well out of getting on the property ladder early a decade ago, although his current home, which cost £230,000 two years ago, is now worth £205,000. He would like a retirement income of £20,000 in today's terms, yet to achieve that he is going to have to save more than £350 a month in a pension, assuming he receives a state pension of £7,000 a year. If he delays starting to save by five years, the amount he will need to save will rise to £456 a month.

John said: 'Financial products are more complicated now than when my father was a young man. These days you have to make your own choices, whereas in his day it was all done for you. For many years I was not offered a pension because I was not senior enough, and, for those periods when I have been, I have thought I would not be around with this employer long enough to make it worth it.

'The other big difference from my father's generation is that credit was easy when I was in my teens and early twenties. Everything was supposed to be OK because the equity in your house was supposed to pay for it all. I had a fantastic time on credit cards and there was no warning that you needed to rein it in. Then the credit crunch came. The monthly mortgage payments are really biting now and the idea of forking out even more on a pension will leave us really stretched.'

But John accepts that the longer he leaves it, the harder saving for a decent retirement will be. 'For years I thought I could rely on property for my long-term future. I now accept that a pension may be what I need to do,' he said.

18 June 2012

⇨ The above article originally appeared in *The Telegraph*. Please visit www.telegraph.co.uk for further information on this and other subjects.

Care in crisis 2012

Summary from the 2012 report by Age UK.

The recent history of funding

⇨ There is serious underspend on older people's social care. Spend on older people's care stagnated and then decreased between 2005-06 and 2011-12. Yet the number of people aged over 85, the age group who are most likely to need care, has increased by over 250,000 since 2004-05.[1] As a result each year unmet need has increased as people are excluded from accessing services or see their care packages reduced.

⇨ Councils have cut back on their service provision. In 2009-10 the total hours of support purchased by local authorities for older people fell from 2 million to 1.85 million.[2]

⇨ Provision of care is more restricted than ever. In 2005 half of councils provided support to people assessed as having 'moderate' needs, but in 2011 the figure fell to 18 per cent.[3]

⇨ Many older people miss out altogether, remaining outside of the state care system. Today of 2 million older people in England with care-related needs nearly 800,000 receive no support from public or private sector agencies.[4]

⇨ The financial demands on older people who receive care are increasing. In real terms, charges were £150 per year more in 2010-11 than in 2009-10 for each older person using local authority care services and £360 more than in 2008-09.

1 Source: ONS Population Estimates, mid-2004 – mid 2010 (accessed via ONS website).

2 www.ic.nhs.uk/statistics-and-data-collections/ social-care/adult-social-care-information

3 State of Care report 2010-11, Care Quality Commission, www.cqc.org.uk/stateofcare2010-11.cfm

4 Forder and Fernandez (2011) The cost of social care for older people: the importance of unit cost growth. PSSRU report for Age UK

The spending decisions taken by the Coalition Government

⇨ Funding for frontline services has not been protected. Councils have reduced their spending on older people's social care by £671 million in real terms in the year between 2010-11 and 2011-12.[5] This is a decrease of over eight per cent.[6]

⇨ Additional money from the NHS has not filled the gap. Even after adding the £330 million transferred from PCTs to the amount spent by local authorities, the overall effect is still a real decrease in spending on older people's social care of £341 million or around 4.5 per cent.

⇨ Taking into account growing demand as well, the gap is even greater. In order to maintain the care system at the same level as in 2010 (before current spending cuts), expenditure on older people's social care should be £7.8 billion in 2011-12. But this year total spending it is only £7.3 billion. Even making allowances for efficiency gains, this has left a total shortfall of £500 million.

Paying for care reform

⇨ Just to maintain the status quo a steady increase in funding will be needed. By 2015 we should be spending £9.4 billion per year to maintain the 2010 status quo and stop the system getting any worse. That is £2.1 billion more than was spent this year.

⇨ Provision should be extended to support people who fund their

5 2011-12 prices calculated using the RPI (all items), averages for financial year 2010-11 and 2011-12 (to August 2011).

6 Analysing only spending by councils with adult social service responsibility (CASSRs), this decrease is 4.9%.

own care. Age UK supports implementation of the Dilnot Commission's proposals for care reform, in particular measures that mitigate the risk of incurring catastrophic costs and support people who self-fund to plan in advance. The Dilnot reforms would cost an estimated £2.2 billion in 2015.

⇨ Meeting moderate needs also needs to be factored in to the overall sums for reform. Extending the reach of the formal care system should be a key objective for the Government. Costing this additional provision should be a priority.

'Of two million older people in England with care-related needs nearly 800,000 receive no support'

The architecture of reform

Age UK has set out seven key building blocks that are critical to the success of care reform.

1. Care and support must be available to everyone who needs it:

⇨ Government should introduce a national eligibility threshold set at moderate.

⇨ People should be entitled to an assessment that fully considers their individual needs, as proposed by the Law Commission. No one should ever be refused care without full consideration of their needs based on a proper assessment.

⇨ People should be able to take existing assessments with them when they move from one local authority to another (portable assessments).

2. Care and support services should be high quality and safe:

⇨ Care regulation needs to be strengthened: the regulator should take a strong monitoring role and be given an enhanced quality improvement role to support providers to get better; services should also be properly overseen by local authorities where they arrange support.

⇨ Local authorities should become more responsive by involving service users and the public in planning and delivering services.

⇨ Local authorities must plan services strategically to ensure a choice of good quality services is available.

⇨ The Government should support the introduction of a clear and transparent quality scheme so that people can judge in advance how good a service or provider is.

⇨ Where local authorities must support users to choose how they receive their services if an individual chooses not to use a cash payment to meet their care needs, services should still be organised on their behalf.

3. Services should support people to live safely and with self-respect:

⇨ A reformed system must be founded on a clear principle that care and support enable people to live with dignity, to be as independent as possible, to be part of a community and to maintain family and social relationships.

⇨ Local authorities should be responsible for ensuring that care and support services are available to support someone at all stages of their needs, to manage transitions and following major life-changing events.

4. Preparing in advance for care should be straightforward:

⇨ People must be able to obtain free information and advice about the care system.

⇨ Information about financial products should be independent and appropriately regulated.

⇨ Measures that enable people to take steps to delay the need to use care services must form part of a reformed system.

5. Care should be funded in a fair and transparent way:

⇨ The Government should implement the funding recommendations set out by the Dilnot Commission, including the introduction of a £35,000 cap and £100,000 mean test thresholds.

⇨ Deferred payments should be available in every local authority area so that people do not have to sell their home when they move into residential care.

6. The system should be clear and easy to understand:

⇨ The Government should implement the recommendations of the Law Commission for a single social care statute.

⇨ Local authorities must continue to have clear care management duties, including responsibilities to arrange care for people who qualify for support.

⇨ People must have appropriate support available to negotiate the system, including access to advocacy and new roles such as support brokers and care navigators.

⇨ New legislation must make clear which agency has ultimate statutory responsibility for the care provided and is responsible for any charges applied.

7. No family member or friend who acts as a carer should be forced to sacrifice health, career, social life or future economic security:

⇨ Carers must be given a right to support following an assessment of their needs as proposed by the Law Commission.

⇨ The benefits system should be reformed so that there is adequate financial support available for carers.

⇨ The above information is reprinted with kind permission from Age UK. Please visit www.ageuk.org.uk.

Social care: how it could be paid for in the future

Based on the leaflet Fairer care funding: Reforming the funding of adult social care.

What is social care?

Social care supports people who can't manage by themselves.

Social care helps people with everyday tasks they can't do on their own and makes sure they can take an active part in life. For example, people may need help to:

⇨ live in their home

⇨ get washed and dressed

⇨ go out and about

⇨ meet friends.

You may need social care because you are older or because you have an illness or disability which makes it difficult for you to look after yourself.

You may be looked after by a family member or by someone who is paid to look after you.

You may also need somewhere safe to live.

People who need social care also often need healthcare, but healthcare is paid for in a different way. Healthcare is given to you free by the NHS. This article is not about changing healthcare.

Why do we need to change the way social care is paid for?

People are living longer. This is something to celebrate. However, there is not enough money to pay for all the people who will need social care in future. At the moment, some people have to pay for social care if they need it and some don't. Some people need to sell their home to pay for their care, while other people don't. Many people think this is unfair.

A lot of people are worried about how they will pay for social care if they need it now or in the future. People would like to be able to plan in advance how they will pay for care, but they can't because they don't know how much it will cost.

The Government wants to find a better, fairer way to pay for adult social care in the future.

In 2010, the Government created a Commission on Funding of Care and Support to help it decide what to do.

What is the Commission on Funding of Care and Support?

The Commission on Funding of Care and Support was created by the Government. It is not part of the Government. This means that the Commission can say what it thinks – it does not have to agree with the Government.

The Commission's job is to look at how adult social care is paid for now and suggest a better way of paying for care in the future. It is not looking at social care for children.

You can see the Commission's full report at www.dilnotcommission.dh.gov.uk Remember that the Commission has only suggested a new plan to pay for social care. The Government still has to decide whether or not it agrees with this plan.

How the new plan to pay for social care could work

⇨ People who have very little money will not have to pay anything.

⇨ The Commission thinks people who need care before they are 18 should not have to pay anything during their life.

⇨ The Commission also thinks people who need care before they are 40 should not need to pay anything during their life.

⇨ Everyone else who can afford to do so will have to pay up to around £35,000 of their care costs.

⇨ After people have paid £35,000, they will not have to pay any more for their care. The Government will pay all their care costs after that.

This plan could help more people plan ahead and save for their care needs. It will mean people will not have to worry as much about how to pay for their care if they become ill.

Changes to the means test for people who need care

Local councils assess people who need care to work out how much money they have and how much they should pay for their care. This is called a means test.

At the moment, the means test is set at £23,250. If you are in a care home now and you have more than £23,250 (including the value of your home), you may not get any help from the Government with your care costs.

We think the Government should change the means test to £100,000 for people in a care home. This would mean you would be able to spend more of your own money on yourself.

How will the new plan affect me if I need care in the future?

If you need care in the future, you will not need to worry about how much you might have to pay. If you do not have enough money, you will not need to pay for your care. If you do have money, you may need to pay up to £35,000. After that, the Government will pay for your care. It is a good idea to plan ahead how you will pay for care if you need it later in your life. You could:

⇨ put aside money now which you can use later if you need care

⇨ talk to someone about how you can plan for paying for your care, if you have money already or if you own a house.

If you are worried about paying for your care later in your life, it's a good idea to talk to someone about it now. You could talk to:

⇨ a family member or friend

- the Citizens Advice Bureau, which is there to help people decide what to do about problems. You can look up your nearest Citizens Advice Bureau in your telephone directory or on the Internet

- your local social services department

- people who help care for you.

What happens if I can't pay for my care?

If you don't have enough money to pay for your care, the Government will pay for your care, which is what happens now.

What happens next?

We have told the Government how we think the way care is paid for should change. The Government needs to decide whether it agrees and how quickly to make changes to the way care is paid for. Once this decision is made, the Government will tell anyone who is affected by the changes.

How can I find out more?

You may want to know more about these changes. You could talk to:

- a family member or friend

- the Citizens Advice Bureau

- your local council

- your care worker

- your doctor.

July 2011

- Information from the Commission on Funding of Care and Support and is reprinted with permission from the Department of Health. Visit www.dilnotcommission. dh.gov.uk for further information on this and other subjects.

Government to implement Dilnot care reforms 'as soon as it is able'

Information from Money Marketing.

By Paul Thomas

Health secretary Jeremy Hunt says the Government is committed to implementing the Dilnot cap on social care costs 'as soon as we are able'.

The Dilnot Commission's report, published in July 2011, called for a cap on individuals' lifetime contributions to social care costs of between £25,000 and £50,000, with £35,000 the recommended figure. When that cap is reached, people would be eligible for full state support. The cap would not cover 'hotel costs' of care funding such as accommodation and food but the commission has called for a standard limit on general living costs in care of between £7,000 and £10,000 a year.

Currently the means-tested threshold where people are required to fund the full costs of their care is £23,250. The commission recommends increasing this to £100,000.

Speaking today at the Conservative Party conference in Birmingham, Hunt said: 'We need to face up to some hard truths about how we are going to pay for social care. I am proud that next year's care and support bill will mean that no one is forced to sell their house in their lifetime to pay for care.

'A historic change. But we also want to go further and implement the Dilnot cap on social care costs as soon as we are able.'

The wording of the speech, and lack of firm commitment to a timetable, is likely to raise concern from industry campaigners who are worried the Government is looking to delay the reforms or kick them into the long grass.

In July, Prime Minister David Cameron accepted the principle of a cap but questioned how the Government might pay the estimated £1.7 bn annual price tag.

The Government has already given a commitment to introduce the Dilnot cap but last month new care services minister Norman Lamb said he is in 'no rush' to push ahead with the reforms. Speaking on Radio 5, the North Norfolk MP Lamb, who replaced Paul Burstow in the recent ministerial reshuffle, refused to give a timetable for the reforms after accepting Dilnot's capped cost principle.

Last month, former care services minister Paul Burstow attacked the Treasury for having no 'sense of urgency' over the reforms.

Symponia joint founder and director Janet Davies says: 'I just wish the Government would do something. There is never any substance behind the comments. We never get a date commitment. We are fast coming to the time when this coalition is coming for election and this will be put on the back burner. The Government needs to be bold and give us a date.'

Partnership director of corporate affairs Jim Boyd says: 'Nothing has really changed. The problem is this has always been subject to finding the funding for this and there is a concern that it will get kicked into the long grass, because it is a very complex issue for politicians to address.

'At the heart of it, it is about a politician telling people, before an election, that people who thought they never had to pay for social care will now have to pay for it. No politician wants to be the one to do that.'

9 October 2012

- Information from Money Marketing. Please visit www. moneymarketing.co.uk for further information.

Age-related illnesses

Doctor Chris Browne gives a brief description of some of the illnesses that can affect people as they get older.

Alzheimer's disease

This is a form of dementia affecting the over-60s. There are more than 500,000 people affected in the UK.

The nerve cells in the brain are slowly destroyed resulting in memory loss and difficulty in completing simple tasks.

It progresses with time and is more likely to affect those with heart disease and poor circulation as well as those with a family history of Alzheimer's.

It is less likely in those who keep their brains active and stimulated and in those with a high Omega 3 diet (fish). So, do lots of brainteasers, crosswords and Sudoku, and eat plenty of fish.

Prescription drugs can slow down the progress of the disease.

For more information visit the Alzheimer's Society website. BUPA has also produced an excellent publication, *Caring for someone with dementia* full of useful and sensitive information.

Angina

Over a million people in the UK suffer from angina, a form of coronary heart disease. It is more common in older people, and affects more women than men.

Angina presents as chest pain or tightness in the chest, most likely to occur when exercising, after a meal or when stressed. The pain can spread to the neck and arms.

An attack of angina doesn't normally last for more than a few minutes. Resting will speed recovery.

Don't ignore angina. Although it is often confused with indigestion, it can be a tell-tale sign of potentially dangerous heart conditions that can lead to a heart attack.

Angina can be treated with drugs and also by various levels of surgery.

Again the British Heart Foundation will give further information.

Cancer

Cancer is a group of cells in the body growing in an uncontrolled way.

One in three of us will at some stage get some form of cancer.

Because of the nature and history of cancer, the fear and dread surrounding the illness is still widespread. However, many cancers are completely curable and most can be treated.

Risk factors are smoking (one in four cancers), unhealthy diet and too much alcohol.

Some cancers are passed down in families. So, eat healthily, stop smoking and choose your parents carefully.

More information is available on Cancer Research UK's website.

Depression

One in four women and one in ten men will suffer from depression at some stage in their lives. This statistic probably under-represents the number of men who suffer from depression...they are less likely to want to admit to having the illness.

Visual impairment in later life

Percentage

People over 75 who will develop cataracts

People over 75 who will develop some symptoms of age-related macular degeneration

People over 65 who have difficulties with their eyesight

People over 75 who have an eye complaint

Source: Later life in the United Kingdom, October 2012, Age UK Group. © Age UK Group

Depression is characterised by low mood, loss of interest in everything, poor sleep, lack of energy, feelings of worthlessness and thoughts of suicide.

There are many treatments apart from drugs – counselling, exercise and alternative and natural therapies.

MIND is the charity that supports and advises those with depression and other mental illnesses.

Diabetes

Diabetes is the lack of insulin that controls the level of sugar in the blood.

Type 1 affects children and young adults and requires insulin therapy.

Type 2 is much more common and starts slowly, affects older people and is generally controlled with diet and/or pills.

Two million in the UK are known to have it and it is likely that 750,000 have diabetes without knowing it. The most obvious symptoms are tiredness, excessive thirst and frequent urination, so if you seem to have a permanent hangover, see your doctor.

Causes are heredity and lifestyle, especially obesity.

Visit Diabetes UK's website for further information.

Hearing loss

Half of all over-60s are deaf or hard of hearing – that's about nine million in the UK.

Hearing loss can be due to loss of conduction of sound – wax, ear infection and ear damage causing a hole in the ear drum, or due to nerve malfunction – age, noise damage and some drugs.

If people complain that they have to shout at you, or you have the sound up too high on the TV, get an ear check - it may only be wax.

Treatment with hearing aids or surgery is getting more sophisticated and effective.

Royal National Institute for the Deaf's website has some sound information as does Deafness Research UK.

Heart and circulatory disease

More people die from heart disease in the UK than any other cause. About 7.5 per cent of men and 4.5 per cent of women are affected and the numbers increase with age.

The underlying cause is furring up of the major arteries (blood tubes) in the heart and elsewhere with fat and cholesterol.

Symptoms

⇨ Angina (see above). This is due to narrowing of the blood vessels that supply oxygen to the heart muscle. It causes central 'heavy' chest pain that comes on with exertion.

⇨ Ankle swelling. When the heart muscle pumps blood less effectively, the body compensates by keeping more fluid in the circulation and this results in swollen ankles.

⇨ Breathlessness. Another symptom of reduced heart function is breathlessness from exertion, caused by an increase of blood in the lungs that makes them stiffer, so breathing is harder.

⇨ Mini stroke. If the circulation in the brain is furred up, brain function can be impaired. Sometimes this shows as a short-lived episode of weakness down one side or difficulty with speech. Loss of recent memory is another symptom.

⇨ Raised blood pressure. Normally caused by the heart pumping harder to force blood through furred up blood vessels. Symptoms include headaches and breathlessness on exertion.

Prevention is better than anything. Having a healthy diet, exercising and a happy life are all well researched measures. Many drugs are also available to manage heart and circulatory disease and there are lots of surgical interventions to reduce the dangers.

More information is available from the British Heart Foundation.

Impaired vision

Vision: the process of seeing and beholding beauty. And quite often, the older you get, the more the vision becomes impaired. Maybe that is why the older we get, the less interested we are in beholding beauty. Or maybe not...

The eye is a complex mechanism – for most of our evolution, it has only had to work for 30 or 40 years, so it is understandable that it gets a bit worn when we reach older age.

For most of us, wearing the right spectacles or contact lenses enable us to see properly and counter the effects of wear. However, many of us are not using the right glasses or lenses, because we don't have our eyes checked regularly enough.

But with age also come more serious illnesses that affect our eyes.

Osteoarthritis

Two million people see their GP for this every year in the UK. There are different forms of arthritis but osteoarthritis, or 'wear and tear' arthritis is the most common. Joints become stiff and painful and get misshapen and knobbly.

Risk factors include being overweight, being inactive, previous joint injury especially high level sports injury. Women are more affected than men.

Prevention means losing weight and being active. Swimming is especially beneficial. Treatment consists of pain killers, physical therapy and replacement surgery.

See Arthritis Care's website for further information.

Osteoporosis

One in two women and one in five men over the age of 50 will break a bone, mainly because of osteoporosis, the increasing brittleness of bones.

Although fractures can occur in different parts of the body, the wrist, hip and spine are most commonly affected, normally because these take the impact when a person falls.

Having osteoporosis does not automatically mean that your bones will break, nor does it generally slow or stop the healing process, but there is a greater risk of fracture.

Osteoporosis can be delayed by building up a bone 'bank' through weight-bearing exercise and diet during the early adult years.

Even so, at any age a good diet rich in calcium and minerals, is recommended, as is taking exercise... being fit and active will reduce fragility and the chances of falls.

Drugs to strengthen bones are available for those at highest risk of fracture.

More information is available at the National Osteoporosis Society.

Strokes

Strokes are more common in people over 55, and the risk continues to rise with age as arteries harden and become 'furred' by a build-up of cholesterol and other debris.

You are more likely to suffer from a stroke if it runs in the family. Those from Asian, African and African-Caribbean communities are at greater risk of a stroke.

The most common type of stroke is a blockage caused by a clot blocking an artery that carries blood to the brain.

Also common is haemorrhagic stroke when a blood vessel bursts, causing bleeding into the brain.

Symptoms of a stroke are very sudden. They include numbness, weakness or paralysis on one side of the body; slurred speech; blurred vision or loss of sight; confusion; unsteadiness; and a severe headache.

Medical conditions that contribute to the risk of strokes are high blood pressure, diabetes, obesity and heart disease/circulatory problems.

Lifestyle choices are also contributory so stop smoking, cutback on fatty foods, eat plenty of fruit and vegetables, have your blood pressure checked regularly, exercise regularly and avoid heavy drinking.

Visit the Stroke Association for more information.

⇨ The above information is reprinted with kind permission from My Last Song. Please visit www.mylastsong.com for further information on this and other subjects.

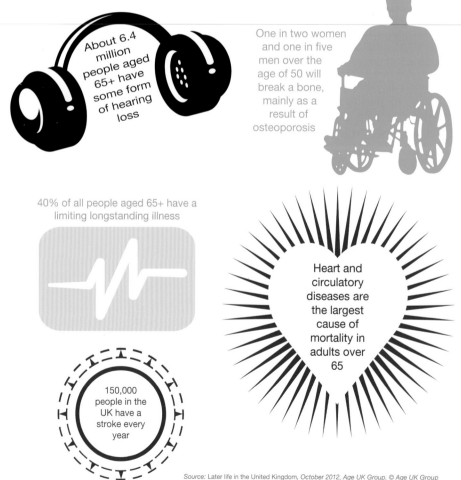

About 6.4 million people aged 65+ have some form of hearing loss

One in two women and one in five men over the age of 50 will break a bone, mainly as a result of osteoporosis

40% of all people aged 65+ have a limiting longstanding illness

Heart and circulatory diseases are the largest cause of mortality in adults over 65

150,000 people in the UK have a stroke every year

Source: Later life in the United Kingdom, October 2012, Age UK Group. © Age UK Group

Top ten tips for better ageing

We know it's not just about living longer, it's about living healthily and happily for longer. Follow our top ten tips for ageing better together.

1. Exercise

You don't have to join an exercise class or the gym – things like gardening, playing tennis or bowls, or going for a brisk walk can be just as effective.

Just make sure you check with your doctor if you have a condition or haven't exercised in a while.

2. Eat a healthy diet

Eat plenty of fruit and vegetables – aim for five portions a day.

Too much salt increases your risk of high blood pressure and stroke. Check food labels for the salt content, particularly in processed meats, savoury snacks, biscuits, bacon, soups and ready meals.

Too much saturated fat raises cholesterol and increases the risk of heart disease and stroke. Foods high in saturated fat include biscuits, cakes, pastries, sausages, meat pies, fatty meat and cheese.

Don't drink too much alcohol. Know how many units you are drinking, and speak to your GP if you find yourself regularly having a drink to help you cope.

3. Don't smoke

It's never too late to feel the benefits of giving up smoking. Ask your GP or pharmacist about local one-to-one or group support and anti-smoking medication.

You can also find out more online at NHS' smokefree site.

4. Engage socially with others

Why not volunteer with Age UK? It doesn't matter how much or little time you have – with more than 170 local Age UKs, as well as around 500 shops, you can get involved in your local community and meet new people.

Age UK volunteers do everything from gardening and driving to visiting people living alone. You could be serving customers and helping to dress the window in one of our shops.

Or you could work behind the scenes sorting through donations or helping with basic administration.

We also welcome book or antique enthusiasts in our shops to help price donations. With your help we can deliver more services to people in later life.

5. Have a positive attitude about ageing

Research shows that older people who have a positive attitude to ageing, and who work with the changes it brings, tend to have better health and live longer than those who see only the negatives.

Devoting time to old friends and favourite hobbies is important – but remember to explore new interests too. It's easy to meet new friends, try new activities or share something you enjoy in your local area.

Age UK supports more than 85 Friendship Centres across England and works with a network of 600 independent forums of older people.

6. Get regular health check-ups

Speak to your GP if there is a family history of heart disease, high blood pressure, diabetes, osteoporosis or glaucoma. This helps identify any problems before symptoms arise.

Don't ignore invitations for a flu jab or cancer screening. NHS screening programmes for breast, bowel and cervical cancer are there to pick up problems at an early stage.

7. Protect your eyes

Take advantage of free NHS sight tests if you're eligible. Have your eyes checked every two years, or annually if you are aged 70 or over.

8. Avoid excessive sun exposure

While it's good to get outside and enjoy good weather, it's important that you take precautions when the sun is out.

There are odd occasions when very high temperatures and humidity can

present a risk to health, and many of us can be particularly susceptible to heat-related illness.

9. Get sufficient good-quality sleep

Getting a decent night's sleep isn't just about beating tiredness. Good-quality sleep has additional health benefits, such as reducing your risk of depression, lowering inflammation, helping stress and even improving your heart health.

10. Pay attention to your pension, and get expert financial advice

There's never been a more important time to get your finances checked out. Your pension could be working harder for you and your savings may not be in the best place.

Talking to an independent financial adviser is the best way to get impartial advice about your money matters and ensure that you are getting everything that you're entitled to.

⇨ The above information is reprinted with kind permission from Age UK. Please visit www.ageuk.org.uk for further information.

© Age UK Group

What is dementia?

Factsheet produced by the Alzheimer's Society.

The term 'dementia' describes a set of symptoms which include loss of memory, mood changes, and problems with communication and reasoning. These symptoms occur when the brain is damaged by certain diseases, including Alzheimer's disease and damage caused by a series of small strokes.

Dementia is progressive, which means the symptoms will gradually get worse. How fast dementia progresses will depend on the individual person and what type of dementia they have. Each person is unique and will experience dementia in their own way. It is often the case that the person's family and friends are more concerned about the symptoms than the person may be themselves.

Symptoms of dementia may include the following:

⇨ Loss of memory: this particularly affects short-term memory, for example forgetting what happened earlier in the day, not being able to recall conversations, being repetitive or forgetting the way home from the shops. Long-term memory is usually still quite good.

⇨ Mood changes: people with dementia may be withdrawn, sad, frightened or angry about what is happening to them.

⇨ Communication problems: including problems finding the right words for things, for example describing the function of an item instead of naming it.

In the later stages of dementia, the person affected will have problems carrying out everyday tasks and will become increasingly dependent on other people.

What causes dementia?

There are several diseases and conditions that result in dementia. These include:

⇨ Alzheimer's disease: The most common cause of dementia. During the course of the disease the chemistry and structure of the brain change, leading to the death of brain cells. Problems of short-term memory are usually the first noticeable sign.

⇨ Vascular dementia: If the oxygen supply to the brain fails due to vascular disease, brain cells are likely to die and this can cause the symptoms of vascular dementia. These symptoms can occur either suddenly, following a stroke, or over time through a series of small strokes.

⇨ Dementia with Lewy bodies: This form of dementia gets its name from tiny abnormal structures that develop inside nerve cells. Their presence in the brain leads to the degeneration of brain tissue. Symptoms can include disorientation and hallucinations, as well as problems with planning, reasoning and problem solving. Memory may be affected to a lesser degree. This form of dementia shares some characteristics with Parkinson's disease.

⇨ Fronto-temporal dementia (including Pick's disease): In fronto-temporal dementia, damage is usually focused in the front part of the brain. At first, personality and behaviour changes are the most obvious signs.

Rarer causes of dementia

There are many other rarer diseases that may lead to dementia, including progressive supranuclear palsy, Korsakoff's syndrome, Binswanger's disease, HIV/AIDS, and Creutzfeldt Jakob disease (CJD). Some people with multiple sclerosis, motor neurone disease, Parkinson's disease and Huntington's disease may also develop dementia as a result of disease progression.

Mild cognitive impairment

Some individuals may have noticed problems with their memory, but a doctor may feel that the symptoms are not severe enough to warrant a diagnosis of Alzheimer's disease or another type of dementia, particularly if a person is still managing well. When this occurs, some doctors will use the term 'mild cognitive impairment' (MCI). Recent research has shown that individuals with MCI have an increased risk of developing dementia. The conversion rate from MCI to Alzheimer's is ten to 20 per cent each year, so a diagnosis of MCI does not always mean that the person will go on to develop dementia.

Who gets dementia?

⇨ There are about 800,000 people in the UK with dementia.

⇨ Dementia mainly affects people over the age of 65 and the likelihood increases with age. However, it can affect younger people: there are over 17,000 people in the UK under the age of 65 who have dementia.

⇨ Dementia can affect men and women.

⇨ Scientists are investigating the genetic background to dementia. It does appear that in a few rare cases the diseases that cause dementia can be inherited. Some people with a particular genetic make-up have a higher risk than others of developing dementia.

Can dementia be cured?

Most forms of dementia cannot be cured, although research is continuing into developing drugs, vaccines and other treatments. Drugs have been developed that can temporarily alleviate some of the symptoms of some types of dementia. These drugs include the three acetylcholinesterase inhibitors:

⇨ Aricept (donepezil hydrochloride)

⇨ Exelon (rivastigmine)

⇨ Reminyl (galantamine).

How can I tell if I have dementia?

Many people fear they have dementia, particularly if they think that their memory is getting worse or if they have known someone who has had the illness. Becoming forgetful does not necessarily mean that you have dementia: memory loss can be an effect of ageing, and it can also be a sign of stress or depression. In rare cases, dementia-like symptoms can be caused by vitamin deficiencies and/or a brain tumour. If you are worried about yourself, or someone close to you, it is worth discussing your concerns with your GP.

Diagnosing dementia

It is very important to get a proper diagnosis. A diagnosis will help the doctor rule out any illnesses that might have similar symptoms to dementia, including depression. Having a diagnosis may also mean it is possible to be prescribed drugs for Alzheimer's disease. Whether you are someone with dementia or a carer, a diagnosis can help with preparing and planning for the future.

Dementia can be diagnosed by a doctor – either a GP or a specialist. The specialist may be a geriatrician (a doctor specialising in the care of older people), a neurologist (someone who concentrates on diseases of the nervous system) or a psychiatrist (a mental health specialist). The doctor may carry out a number of tests to check basic thinking processes and the ability to perform daily tasks. They may request further tests, such as a brain scan or a more in-depth assessment of memory, concentration and thinking skills.

Can dementia be prevented?

At present, it is not clear what causes most of the diseases that lead to dementia. It is not clear what can be done to prevent dementia itself but the evidence does indicate that a healthy diet and lifestyle may help protect against dementia. In particular, exercising regularly, avoiding fatty foods, not smoking, drinking alcohol in moderation and keeping mentally and socially active into old age may help to reduce the risk of developing vascular dementia and Alzheimer's disease.

⇨ The above information is reprinted with kind permission from Alzheimer's Society. Please visit www.alzheimers.org.uk for further information.

© 2012 Alzheimer's Society

Dementia in later life

Dementia costs the UK approximately £23 billion a year, about twice as much as cancer

One in three people over 65 will die from some form of dementia

Dementia is one of the main causes of disability in later life

There are an estimated 36 million dementia sufferers worldwide ... 27 million are thought to be undiagnosed

Over 820,000 people were estimated to be suffering from late onset dementia in the UK in 2010

Source: Later life in the United Kingdom, October 2012, Age UK Group. © Age UK Group

Are you worried about dementia?

63% of UK adults are worried about the condition.

Nearly two thirds of UK adults are worried about dementia, according to our poll commissioned jointly by Alzheimer's Society and Saga Homecare, published this week to coincide with Dementia Awareness Week™.

⇨ 63% of UK adults say they are worried about dementia in some way (while 24% said they weren't worried).

⇨ 61% are worried about either themselves or someone they know developing dementia in later life.

⇨ Yet despite their fears, and only 21% thinking they have a good knowledge of dementia, less than a fifth (16%) of people want to know more about the condition.

⇨ Although 18-24-year-olds are the most keen to learn more (25%) in comparison to only 15% of people aged 55 or over.

⇨ Only 18% of people realise dementia is a terminal illness.

⇨ And just 6% of people have a plan in place if a family member were to develop dementia (this includes only 7% of people aged 55 and over).

The poll, which questioned 4,276 UK adults over 18, found that those aged 55 or over are the most worried (66%) but dementia is even worrying over half of younger people aged 18 to 24 (61%).

Women are much more concerned about dementia than men, with 70% worrying about the condition in some way, in comparison to 56% of men.

Separate Alzheimer's Society research shows that of the 800,000 people in the UK who have a form of dementia, more than half have Alzheimer's disease.

'Biggest challenge today'

Jeremy Hughes, Chief Executive of Alzheimer's Society, commented on the YouGov poll, saying that 'dementia is the biggest challenge facing the UK today so it's not surprising that people are so worried. There is currently no cure and people aren't getting the care they deserve. However we know that with the right support people can live well with the condition for a number of years.

'This Dementia Awareness Week™ we need to stop worrying and start understanding dementia. Whether you have five minutes or half an hour, please take some time to learn about dementia. Only through knowing more will we ensure that the people with the condition are treated with the dignity and respect they deserve.'

John Ivers, Chief Executive of Saga Homecare, which provides care at home for people who want to maintain their independence, said: 'We are delighted to be partnering with Alzheimer's Society in raising awareness of dementia. Saga Homecare has extensive experience of providing ongoing support to people with this condition and we are harnessing our resources to help Alzheimer's Society make an impact with this worthwhile campaign.'

22 May 2012

⇨ The above information is reprinted with kind permission from YouGov. Please visit www.yougov.co.uk for further information.

Depression in later years

Depression is one of the most common illnesses in older people. Here we look at possible reasons, and practical tips.

Experiencing change

As we approach old age, most of us are going through a significant amount of change. Our children have their own families and can seem distant and independent which is often very different from our own family life. This can mean we have to endure the hugely stressful experience of not seeing our grandchildren because of family conflict or having to take on the responsibility for our grandchildren because their parents cannot cope.

Other complex changes include retirement, if in work, and having to face worrying financial circumstances. There can be a reduced sense of purpose and loss of identity due to not being in the workplace. You may feel very isolated, especially if you are living alone. Our health can become an issue too, and we have to face regularly the serious illness and or death of our friends, family and even our partner.

The effects of depression

Depression is not a normal or necessary part of aging. This is not something you have to endure on your own. If depression goes untreated, it can affect our ability to keep up with treatment for other conditions, interfere with recovery from physical illnesses, increase physical decline and make it harder to function day to day. Depression can be alleviated through medical and psychotherapeutic interventions and there is a range of support to help you through your unhappiness. There is no stigma in seeking help.

What are the signs of depression?

If you learn how to spot the signs of depression and find effective ways to help early on, you are well on the way to living with a more positive and happy outlook. These are just some of the feelings which are a cause for concern:

⇨ Sadness

⇨ Fatigue

⇨ Abandoning or losing interest in hobbies or other pleasurable pastimes

⇨ Social withdrawal and isolation (reluctance to be with friends, engage in activities, or leave home)

⇨ Weight loss; loss of appetite

⇨ Sleep disturbances (difficulty falling asleep or staying asleep, oversleeping, or daytime sleepiness)

⇨ Loss of self-worth (worries about being a burden, feelings of worthlessness, self-loathing)

⇨ Increased use of alcohol or other drugs

⇨ Fixation on death; suicidal thoughts or attempts. The suicide rate in the UK is highest in the older population, particularly in older men.

If you experience even a few of these over several weeks, you should seek help.

Treatment for depression

Depression treatment is just as effective for elderly adults as it is for younger people. Therapy, support groups, and medication can all help relieve symptoms. Research has shown that a combination of psychotherapy and antidepressants is extremely effective in preventing depression from recurring.

Antidepressant treatment

Antidepressant treatments help ease the symptoms of depression. These can take between two and four weeks to begin to help and sometimes you may find that the treatment chosen does not agree with you, or has strong side effects. Your GP should work with you to find the best medication for you.

Counselling and therapy

Studies have found that therapy works just as well as medication in relieving mild to moderate depression. And unlike antidepressants, therapy also addresses the underlying causes of the depression.

⇨ Supportive counselling can help ease loneliness and the hopelessness of depression.

⇨ Psychotherapy helps people work through stressful life changes, heal from losses, and process difficult emotions.

⇨ Cognitive behavioural therapy (CBT) helps people change negative thinking patterns, deal with problems in healthy ways, and develop better coping skills.

⇨ Support groups for depression, illness, or bereavement connect people with others who are going through the same challenges. They are a safe place to share experiences, advice, and encouragement.

How you can help yourself

If you're depressed, you may not want to do anything or see anybody. But isolation and inactivity only make depression worse. The more active you are – physically, mentally, and socially – the better you'll feel.

Here are some ways to combat and prevent depression:

⇨ Go out more. Try not to stay cooped up at home all day. Go to the park, take a trip to the hairdresser, or have lunch with a friend.

⇨ Limit the time you're alone. If you can't get out to socialise, invite loved ones to visit you, or keep in touch over the phone or email.

⇨ Pursue whatever hobbies or pastimes bring or used to bring you joy.

⇨ Volunteer. Helping others is one of

- the best ways to feel better about yourself and regain perspective.

⇨ Get a pet to keep you company.

⇨ Learn a new skill. Pick something that you've always wanted to learn, or that sparks your imagination and creativity.

⇨ Laugh at the world and yourself. Laughter provides a mood boost, so swap humorous stories and jokes with your loved ones, watch a comedy, or read a funny book.

⇨ Maintain a healthy diet. Avoid eating too much sugar and junk food. Choose healthy foods that provide nourishment and energy, and take a daily multivitamin.

⇨ Exercise. Even if you're ill, frail, or disabled, there are many safe exercises you can do to build your strength and boost your mood – even from a chair or wheelchair.

Q & As on depression in older people

My sister died six months ago. Surely my feelings are about loss rather than depression?

Although a grieving person may experience a number of depressive symptoms such as frequent crying and profound sadness, grief is a natural and healthy response to bereavement and other major losses. There is a difference, however, between a normal grief reaction and one that is disabling or unrelenting. While there's no set timetable for grieving, if it doesn't let up over time or extinguishes all signs of joy – laughing at a good joke, brightening in response to a hug, appreciating a beautiful sunset – it may be depression.

I think that I feel low because of the pills I am taking. Could this be the case?

All medications have side effects, but some can actually cause symptoms of depression or make a pre-existing depression worse. Harmful drug interactions or a failure to take a medication as prescribed can also contribute to depression. For elderly individuals with multiple prescriptions, the risk of medication-induced

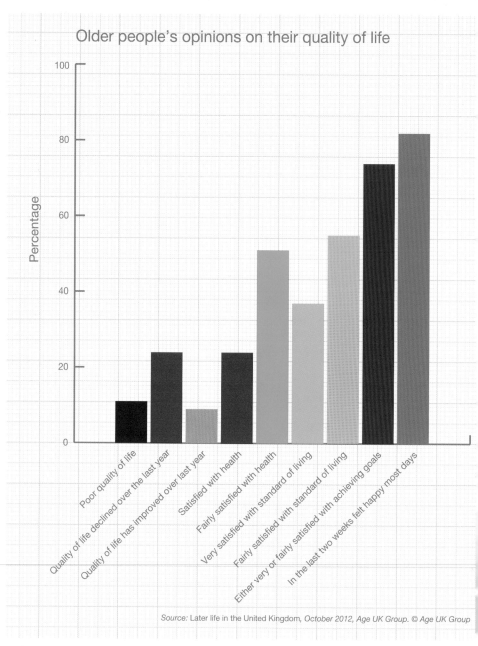

Older people's opinions on their quality of life

Source: Later life in the United Kingdom, October 2012, Age UK Group. © Age UK Group

depression is particularly high. Ask your GP about the side effects of any drugs you are taking.

I can't stop feeling low because I am in agony most days because of my arthritis.

Any medical issues complicating the depression must be addressed and resolved. For example, many older people suffer from chronic pain. Pain that interferes with daily activities can prevent depression recovery, so it must be managed as part of the treatment plan.

I have heard that depression is the start of dementia. Is this right?

The causes for depression in someone who also has dementia are likely to be similar to those for depression. Because the symptoms are often so

similar, an older person with dementia may sometimes be wrongly thought to have depression, and vice versa. It is important to ensure they see their doctor as soon as possible so that an accurate diagnosis can be made.

25 August 2011

This article was kindly provided by The Grandparents' Association. The Grandparents' Association has been working for children since 1987. It's a member organisation and seeks to improve the lives of children by working with and for all grandparents, especially those denied contact; caring for their grandchild full-time; or who have childcare responsibilities for their grandchildren; or are interested in the educational and welfare needs of their grandchildren. Please visit www.grandparents-association.org.uk for further information.

© The Grandparents' Association

Elderly drinking is on the rise

There are new worries about the number of older people who are being admitted to hospital with alcohol-related injuries.

Figures show that elderly drinking is on the rise and health officials are becoming increasingly concerned about this worrying trend.

In the last five years alone there's been a 62% increase in alcohol related hospital admissions for pensioners and it's now estimated that 1.4 million elderly people are drinking much more alcohol than they safely should.

Sarah Wadd who is the director of the Substance Misuse and Ageing Research team at the University of Bedford said: 'We might be on the cusp of an endemic of people drinking problematically in old age.'

What is shocking about the statistics is that over a third of elderly drinkers didn't develop the problem until later in life.

Concerns about money, social isolation, disability and depression make elderly people more susceptible to the lure of drink. Alcohol is the cheapest it's ever been and it's an easy form of temporary comfort when people are stressed or feeling down. It's also a problem that is kept under the radar as so many pensioners drink at home alone, with the tragic consequences not emerging till later.

Elderly people's bodies cannot break down alcohol in the same way as a younger person, so they have got more chance of becoming sick and are more susceptible to liver damage. But not only that, many people will suffer from falls and other accidents in the home as a result of drinking.

The BBC's *Panorama* programme has recently investigated this issue and has found that more than 15% of all elderly people drink every day, compared with just 2% of the under-25s. The figures are quite shocking and BBC research found one of the only ways to tackle the problem would be to make alcohol more expensive.

The Scottish Parliament wants to become the first EU country to have a minimum price for alcohol which would be around 50p per unit. On these figures, a bottle of vodka that currently costs around £9, would be pushed up to £13. The researchers said that an increase like this could save around 50,000 lives over the next ten years as many pensioners would not be able to afford the increase.

Deputy First Minister in Scotland, Nicola Sturgeon said: 'Very cheap cider and very strong cheap lagers are the alcohol products that will get an increase in the price most'

The Scottish plan is certainly one solution but the Government should look further at the root causes of this problem. Issues like social exclusion and poverty are causing major anxiety amongst the elderly population and for many, drinking is an easy escape from it. Elderly drinking is on the rise, and the latest figures show that something more significant needs to be done to stop the problem from getting any worse.

7 September 2012

⇨ The above information is reprinted with kind permission from ANA Nursing. Please visit www.ana-nursing.co.uk for further information.

Recognise and report elder abuse

Information from NI Direct Government Services.

Elder abuse includes actions intending to harm, the harming without intent, and also the neglect that leads to harm of older people. If you're concerned that you might be at risk, or are worried about a friend, relative or client, there are ways to help.

Who is most vulnerable?

People who are physically, emotionally or psychologically frail and dependent on others for care are most at risk of elder abuse. Abuse and neglect can happen in the home, as well as in residential care or nursing homes and hospitals. It can involve care workers, family, neighbours, friends or strangers. People most at risk at home include:

⇨ the socially isolated

⇨ anyone with an illness that affects memory or ability to communicate

⇨ those in a poor relationship with their carer

⇨ those who provide housing, financial or emotional support to their carer

⇨ those who depend on a carer who has drug or alcohol problems.

If you are worried about a friend or relative, there are ways to help. You can go to a social worker, GP or police officer in complete confidence.

How to recognise elder abuse

Elder abuse may happen once or regularly over short or long periods of time. The abuse can be:

⇨ physical – hitting, slapping, pushing, kicking, inappropriate restraint, misuse of medication, inadequate monitoring of prescriptions

⇨ psychological – emotional abuse, threats of harm, threats of leaving or stopping care, lack of human contact, or stopping access to people who can advise or help

⇨ sexual – all unwanted sexual acts

⇨ financial or material, including theft from the abused person, fraud, or coercion regarding wills and any financial transactions

⇨ neglectful – or just not doing something, for example ensuring that the person is eating or is warm and clean

⇨ discriminatory – racist, sexist, exploiting a disability or other forms of harassment or slurs.

There are some tell-tale signs to look for:

⇨ unexplained bruising, fractures, open wounds and welts, and untreated injuries

⇨ poor general hygiene and weight loss

⇨ helplessness and fear – or any sudden change in behaviour

⇨ unexplained changes in a person's finances and material well-being

⇨ questionable financial or legal documents, or the disappearance of those documents.

Reporting abuse

Some types of abuse – including assault (sexual or physical), theft and fraud – are criminal offences that should be reported to the police, social services and the Regulation and Quality Improvement Authority. Such reports may lead to prosecution following a criminal investigation. You may feel too afraid to report abuse, especially if your carer is the abuser, but you are entitled to the protection of the law and to dignity and respect. Anyone concerned about a friend, relative or carer who is being abused needs to take action to prevent further abuse and protect others.

Reporting elder abuse to social services

Local HSC Trusts have social workers dealing specifically with abuse or risk of abuse. If you want to speak to someone, you can phone your local Trust and ask for the adult protection or safeguarding co-ordinator. The adult protection co-ordinator will help you with advice and information, and will ensure action is taken to give people at risk of abuse appropriate protection and support. They can provide a co-ordinating role and investigate what you are concerned about, in discussion with local police and the Health Service.

How to make a formal complaint

The Regulation and Quality Improvement Authority (RQIA) regulates residential care and nursing homes and inspects every home it registers. It also registers homehelp or domiciliary care services. Any registered care provider must, by law, have a complaints procedure. Services have rules about the staff they employ and the standards of care they provide.

⇨ The above information is reprinted with kind permission from NI Direct Government Services. Please visit www.nidirect.gov.uk for further information on this and other subjects.

About loneliness

Information from Campaign to End Loneliness.

Loneliness has been defined by social researchers as 'the subjective, unwelcome feeling of lack or loss of companionship'.

American researchers state that loneliness is an emotion that may have been caused through evolution to ensure humans remain in close contact with each other. Social research over the past few decades has shown that an average of 10% of older people feel 'always' or 'severely' lonely.

This figure has remained the same over decades despite a large number of organisations doing great work to reduce loneliness felt by older people. It should also be noted that in some socio-economic groups and ethnic groups this prevalence of loneliness has been shown as much higher.

In the professional world, loneliness is perceived from a number of different 'expert viewpoints': from social, psychological and medical experts. We know what can cause loneliness, how it affects someone's state of mind and we also know something about the impacts of loneliness on health.

Why is loneliness a problem?

Loneliness is a bigger problem than a simply an emotional experience. Researchers rate loneliness as a similar health risk as lifelong smoking, with links between a lack of social interaction and the onset of degenerative diseases such as Alzheimer's; an illness which costs the NHS an estimated £20 billion a year. Loneliness has also been linked in medical research to heart disease and depression.

Sometimes those who feel lonely don't like to talk about it and currently the health service does not recognise loneliness as a condition they can directly help. If, as a society, we all work to prevent it, the health benefits would be vast. Over the coming months we aim to gather and share information about what works in ending loneliness and what more can be done.

What can be done about loneliness?

There are different types of loneliness: chronic or situational loneliness and social or emotional loneliness. Emotional loneliness is due to the lack of a significant other, while social loneliness is about lacking connections in a wider circle of friends. Researchers suggest that solutions to loneliness should be specific to the needs of individuals:

'lonely older people are different individuals with different needs and expectations' – Professor Mima Cattan.

Friends and family members as well as those working with older people should be sure which type of loneliness the person they are trying to help is feeling and be aware of the individual's wishes, needs and preferences.

What can you do?

⇨ Sign-up to support the Campaign to End Loneliness

⇨ Campaign in your local area – our Loneliness Harms Health campaign asks senior health and care officials to include loneliness in their strategic planning

⇨ Volunteer – with WRVS or Independent Age, or find a local charity through www.Do-It.org. uk.

⇨ Information from Campaign to End Loneliness. Visit www. campaigntoendloneliness.org.uk for further information.

Living alone 'raises death risk in elderly'

Information from NHS Choices.

'Loneliness can shorten your life and make every day activities a struggle,' the *Daily Mail* has reported. The news is based on a US study that examined the relationship between loneliness, 'functional decline' and death of older adults. It found that over six years of follow-up loneliness was associated with death and functional decline, such as reduced mobility and difficulty climbing stairs.

Despite the fact that this study found a link between loneliness, functional decline and death, it does not provide evidence that loneliness actually causes functional decline or death. There is likely to be a complex relationship between reported loneliness and other social, lifestyle, physical and mental health factors. This study was not able to explore this. Although the researchers tried to adjust their analyses for various factors that could have had an influence, it is possible that functional decline and death were due to other factors not measured in the study. Also, both loneliness and functional outcomes were self-reported, which may affect the reliability of the results.

Limited conclusions can be drawn from this relatively small study and the headline that loneliness can shorten your life is misleading.

If you are concerned about the loneliness, isolation or neglect of an elderly person, you may want to talk to your local authority's adult social services department. Anyone with concerns about their mental well-being should talk to their GP. You can find information and support for older people from Age UK.

Where did the story come from?

The study was carried out by researchers from the University of California, US and was funded by grants from the US National Institute on Aging and the Health Resources and Services Administration. The study was published in the peer-reviewed journal *Archives of Internal Medicine*.

The *Mail* gives an accurate representation of this study's findings, although the news does not recognise that this study cannot prove causation due to the complex relationship that is likely to exist between loneliness and other factors that could influence death or functional decline.

A second study in support of the findings and relating to living alone and an increased risk of death from heart disease was reported briefly in the *Daily Express*, and can be found in the same journal.

It should also be noted that the *Daily Express* illustrated the story with a picture of a solitary young man. This is at odds with the study, in which the average subject was female and over 70. The study did not suggest a higher risk of death in the stereotypical young male 'loner', as may have been the impression given in the *Express*.

What kind of research was this?

This was a longitudinal cohort study looking at the relationship between loneliness, functional decline and death in adults older than 60 years.

This type of study looks at the effect that particular exposures or risk factors (in this case, loneliness) have upon groups of people over time. This type of study is normally used to look at the effect of suspected risk factors that cannot be controlled experimentally. Although this study design can demonstrate associations, these studies cannot reliably prove causation due to the inability to control for other factors that could have an influence.

What did the research involve?

The researchers used data from the 2002 Health and Retirement Study, a national US study of people living in the community. The Health and Retirement Study looked at the relationships between health and wealth as people age, including a section on loneliness, stress and social support. The researchers analysed a sub-section of these participants, focusing only on those older than 60 years at time of enrolment (1,604 participants, average age 71). The researchers then examined the relationship between those reporting loneliness and the risk of worsening health and death in the following six years.

Loneliness is the subjective feeling of isolation, not belonging or lacking companionship. Loneliness was only assessed at the time of study enrolment and was determined from a questionnaire that measured three components of loneliness. These were whether participants:

⇨ felt left out

⇨ felt isolated

⇨ lacked companionship.

For each component subjects were asked if they felt that way:

⇨ hardly ever (or never)

⇨ some of the time

⇨ often.

Participants were classified as 'lonely' if they responded 'some of the time' or 'often' to any of the questions.

Researchers looked at the participants' functional decline over a six-year period and whether the participants died in that time. Death was determined from interviews with family members and the National Death Index. Functional decline was determined at study start and at the end of follow-up by looking at four self-reported measures:

⇨ difficulty in an increased number of 'activities of daily living', including dressing, bathing, transferring (for example, getting out of bed), eating and going to the toilet

⇨ difficulty with an increased number of 'upper body tasks' (such as pushing large objects or lifting objects heavier than 10lb)

⇨ a decline in walking

⇨ increased difficulty in stair climbing.

The researchers analysed their results using statistical methods, adjusting the results for demographic differences, education and working status, the number of medical conditions and baseline activities of daily living levels.

What were the basic results?

Of the 1,604 participants, 59% were women, 18% lived alone and 43% reported feeling lonely. The key finding of this study was that loneliness was associated with an increased risk of death during follow-up: 22.8% of those reporting feeling lonely had died, compared with 14.2% of those who did not report being lonely.

Loneliness was also associated with functional decline, with those reporting being lonely more likely to:

⇨ have a decline in activities of daily living (experienced by 24.8% of those reporting feeling lonely compared with 12.5% of those who did not report loneliness, risk ratio 1.59, 95% confidence interval 1.23 to 2.07)

⇨ develop difficulties with 'upper body tasks' (41.5% versus 28.3%, risk ratio 1.28, 95% confidence interval 1.08 to 1.52)

⇨ experience decline in mobility (38.1% versus 29.4%, risk ratio 1.18, 95% confidence interval 0.99 to 1.41)

THANK GOODNESS FOR FRIENDS LIKE YOU!

⇨ have difficulty in climbing stairs (40.8% versus 27.9%, risk ratio 1.31, 95% confidence interval 1.10 to 1.57).

How did the researchers interpret the results?

The researchers conclude that among people over the age of 60, loneliness is a predictor of 'functional decline' and death. Lead researcher Carla Perissinotto is quoted as saying that 'assessment of loneliness is not routine in clinical practice and it may be viewed as beyond the scope of medical practice.

'Our results suggest that questioning older persons about loneliness may be a useful way of identifying elderly persons at risk of disability and poor health outcomes.'

The authors conclude that 'loneliness is a negative feeling that would be worth addressing even if the condition had no health implications'.

Conclusion

Overall, this relatively small study provides limited evidence that loneliness reported by those older than 60 years is associated with functional decline (disability) and an increased risk of death. It does not prove that loneliness causes functional decline or death. There is likely to be a complex relationship between reported loneliness and other social, lifestyle, physical and mental health factors, and the study is not able to explore this. Though the researchers attempted to adjust their analyses for various factors that could have had an influence, it is possible that functional decline and death were due to other factors that were not measured.

19 June 2012

⇨ The above information is reprinted with kind permission from NHS Choices. Please visit www.nhs.uk for further information.

Can technology help us to support the ageing population?

How we care for our relatives and neighbours could be the greatest challenge facing society.

Over the coming decades, older people face a perfect storm. They will reach retirement age when people are living longer than ever, pensions are in crisis and national government and local authorities are facing unprecedented spending cuts. Serious medical conditions, and the socio-economic challenges resulting from ageing, are on the rise – with dementia causing particular distress to many older people and their families, and isolation proving a persistent curse.

This crisis will only deepen over time. Tax revenues continue to diminish and state-led solutions, which for the past 70 years have provided comfort, dignity and care for people in old age, are not going to provide all the answers in future, no matter which political party is in power.

At a time when many older and middle-aged people should be looking ahead to the period of their greatest opportunity, they are in fact instead facing the era of gravest threat.

Thankfully, government departments, local authorities and charitable trusts are alert to these challenges, and are making efforts to find solutions. From the Department of Health to charities and organisations like Nesta, UnLtd and the Calouste Gulbenkian Foundation, funders and researchers are embracing innovation and taking punts on ideas – seeking the concepts, technologies and partnerships that could be improved and rolled out more widely in the future, and at low cost.

Spurred by research indicating that people aged between 50 and 74 are more likely to volunteer, UnLtd has a programme to increase the number of social enterprises created by older people, for older people.

It is hoped that user-led entrepreneurialism will inspire dozens of hyper-local schemes, each responding to a particular need in specific communities. That must be a blueprint for the national Government's approach, too – unleashing new projects, learning from the best, and applying the skills, expertise and human interaction that's so important for a healthy life.

In particular, entrepreneurs are harnessing the power of digital technology to bring people together to develop local solutions to global problems.

Grannynet is a website that supports a community of more than 3,000 grandmothers. It is a vibrant digital community that also provides access to offline courses for grandparents to get to grips with modern parenting methods. Its founder, Verity Gill, says the site is a place 'to exchange the positive experiences of grandparenting and also a course of support through the bad bits'.

Cura, a new technology platform set up in Wiltshire, is a website that helps families and friends share in the delivery of care for their loved ones. Based on a simple, secure and sharable online calendar, Cura offers respite and provides peace of mind for some of the six million unpaid carers in the UK.

The social enterprise I founded, North London Cares, uses social media to recruit young professionals to help support elderly neighbours with low-level but crucial tasks, such as getting the weekly shopping done, or making that all-important GP appointment. Those small, personal interactions can have a really positive effect in people's lives, providing the connection, comfort, companionship and care many of our more isolated neighbours need.

In the private sector, too, new solutions – often built around new digital techniques – are beginning to appear. Some supermarkets are looking at how to use the web to better serve their older customers, including to reduce the cost of an average food basket. Banks are seeking similar ways to provide a more accessible service to their older customers – developing networks, consulting with customers and responding with improved systems.

In the networked age, that human capital and civic participation represent a potent force waiting to be harnessed for the improved care of our older friends and family. Government, and an enabling mentality across the broader social and private sectors, has a big role to play in unleashing that powerful resource.

Of course, no single group or idea will provide all the solutions. But, given the nature of the problem – and the power of modern technology to connect, enthuse and inspire – I'm confident that in the coming decade we will make strides in deploying technology and human capital to tackle perhaps the greatest challenge of our time: how we care for our older relatives and neighbours in a rapidly ageing society.

3 May 2012

⇨ The above article originally appeared in *The Guardian* and is reprinted with permission. Please visit www.guardian.co.uk for further information.

One in three over-65s in the UK want to be more socially active

Technology Strategy Board highlights the opportunity for innovation to improve later life.

⇨ Over a third of people aged over 65 would like to be more socially active.

⇨ Social confidence increases significantly with age.

⇨ 34 per cent of people aged over 80 consider learning new skills as an important aspect of social life.

⇨ Providing opportunities for older adults to stay connected is key – a fifth of over-65s (21 per cent) say they do not have enough family and friends to stay socially active.

⇨ Campaign from Technology Strategy Board highlights the need for innovation in products, systems and services to create opportunities for older adults to keep in touch with others.

The Technology Strategy Board has released a 'Social Index' of the UK, in terms of age and area, based on how socially active respondents of a poll report their lives to be. The index follows recent research from the Campaign to End Loneliness that revealed how a lack of socialising can be detrimental to the health and quality of life of older adults.

The age index shows a decrease of interaction in later life, yet a common desire to continue to remain socially active with over a third (35 per cent) of people aged over 65 wanting more social interaction than they are able to have.

Having the confidence to socialise increases with age, with only seven per cent of over-65s saying that lack of confidence prevents them from being socially active, compared with nearly a quarter of 18 to 24-year-olds. However, the survey reveals a gap between the desires of older adults and what occurs in reality – nearly seven in ten (69 per cent) of people aged over 80 did not consider themselves socially active, which included simple activities such as 'talking to family and friends on the phone' and 'being part of a group'.

The findings point towards a clear and significant opportunity for the improvement of products, systems and services to create greater ways and means for older adults to stay as socially active as they want to be. The Technology Strategy Board is urging people of all ages to talk about how we can all stay socially active in later life at www.TomorrowTogether.org.uk as part of a campaign to explore the potential for innovation to help us live the way we want to for longer.

With a fifth of adults aged over 65 citing a lack of family and friends as preventing them from being more social, communities have an important role to play – 52 per cent of over-65s say that 'knowing about local events' is key to leading an active social life, the highest of all age groups surveyed. Neighbours also become increasingly important, as 78 per cent of people aged over 80 consider neighbourly chats as being 'socially active' - more than double the percentage of 18 to 24-year-olds (38 per cent).

Jackie Marshall-Cyrus, Lead Specialist on the Technology Strategy Board's Assisted Living Innovation Platform, said: 'As human beings we are intrinsically social creatures and this doesn't change as we age chronologically. There is a clear expectation and desire among people of all ages to remain active and keep in touch with people they care about. This is what social and technological innovation is all about. It must work for everyone and not just for some. These results show that we need to talk about new and creative ways of developing exciting products, services and systems for the future.'

Baroness Sally Greengross, who chairs the All-Party Parliamentary Group on Intergenerational Futures and is Vice Chair of the Group on Dementia and Ageing and Older People, said: 'We are an ageing population and all of us, from school age to senior citizens, must start considering how to make later life in the UK the best it can be. There is a huge opportunity for innovative products and services catered to the needs and wants of older adults – particularly those that help facilitate social interaction. I urge everyone to join the conversation at TomorrowTogether.org.uk.'

Based on how socially active respondents believed their lives to be, the Technology Strategy Board has ranked the major cities in accordance to their levels of social interaction. Oxford leads the way as the most socially active for the over-65s with Sheffield bringing up the rear.

Local initiatives

Local initiatives that connect older adults together or offer intergenerational activities are crucial and the application of technology often plays an important role in these. The Technology Strategy Board has found a selection of interesting and exciting projects in the UK.

One project trains older adults in social entrepreneurship, helping them create and run their own projects. Another uses social media to connect young professionals in transient communities in North London with older adults in need of support, whether that's helping them to cook, taking them to a doctor's appointment or cleaning windows.

17 May 2012

⇨ Information from Mature Times. www.maturetimes.co.uk.

Key facts

⇨ Just one century ago, the average life span in the UK was only 49 years for men and 52 years for women. It is now over 77 for men and nearly 82 for women. (page 1)

⇨ British citizens who reach their 100th birthday receive a telegram from the Queen. In 1952, she sent out just 255 centenary telegrams. In 1999 this had risen to 3,500. (page 1)

⇨ The number of people aged 60 and over has doubled since 1980. In the next five years, the number of people aged 65 and over will outnumber children under the age of five. (page 3)

⇨ Between 2000 and 2050, the proportion of the world's population over 60 years old will double from 11% to 22%. (page 3)

⇨ 65% of all people who are visually impaired are aged 50 and older. (page 4)

⇨ The experience of ageing in the UK is poor compared to other EU countries. (page 8)

⇨ Older people in the UK have the highest rates of loneliness and feel they do not socialise as much as other people their age. (page 8)

⇨ Out of the UK, Germany, the Netherlands and Sweden, Britain's 65s are at the highest risk of poverty. 20% of UK pensioners were at risk of poverty in 2010, compared to only 6% of pensioners in the Netherlands. (page 8)

⇨ Lesbian, gay and bisexual people over 55 are more likely to live alone, and to drink more alcohol more often. Three in five are not confident that social care and support services would be able to understand and meet their needs. (page 10)

⇨ From 1 October 2012, it will be unlawful for service providers to discriminate, victimise, or harass a person because of age. (page 11)

⇨ 60% of older people in the UK agree that age discrimination exists in the daily lives of older people. (page 12)

⇨ 50% of adults agree that once you reach very old age, people tend to treat you like a child. (page 12)

⇨ The International Monetary Fund estimated that the cost of Britain's ageing population could rise to as much as £750 billion. (page 15)

⇨ The highest poverty rates among over-65s were found in Cyprus. (page 17)

⇨ The number of older workers in the UK has almost doubled from 753,000 in 1993 to 1.4 million in 2011. (page 18)

⇨ Councils have reduced their spending on older people's social care by £671 million in real terms in the year between 2010-11 and 2011-12. (page 20)

⇨ Of two million older people in England with care-related needs nearly 800,000 receive no support. (page 20)

⇨ Alzheimer's disease is a form of dementia affecting the over-60s. There are more than 500,000 people affected in the UK. (page 24)

⇨ Heart and circulatory diseases are the largest cause of mortality in adults over 65. (page 26)

⇨ In the last five years alone there's been a 62% increase in alcohol-related hospital admissions for pensioners and it's now estimated that 1.4 million elderly people are drinking much more alcohol than they safely should. (page 33)

⇨ Over a third of people aged over 65 would like to be more socially active. (page 39)

Glossary

Ageing

As you got older your body wears out and experiences some changes. This can include the skin wrinkling and getting thinner, less body fat being stored and your bones and muscles becoming weaker. Your memory may also get worse as you age, and your immune system will not be able to fight disease as easily. This is because the cells in your body gradually become damaged and are no longer able to replace themselves. Although ageing can't be avoided entirely, you can put off the effects of ageing by living a healthy lifestyle.

Ageism

The poor or unfair treatment of someone because of their age. Ageism can affect a person's confidence, job prospects, financial situation and quality of life.

Alzheimer's disease

Alzheimer's disease is a form of dementia that affects the over 60s. There are more than 500,000 people affected in the UK. With Alzheimer's disease, the chemistry and structure of the brain changes, leading to the death of brain cells. As nerve cells in the brain are slowly destroyed, this results in memory loss (problems with short-term memory is usually the first noticeable sign) and difficulty in completing simple tasks. Prescription drugs can slow the progress of the disease. People with a history of heart disease, poor circulation and a family history of Alzheimer's are more likely to be affected. However, people who keep their brains active (such as doing crosswords and playing Sudoku) and have a diet high in Omega 3 (fish) are less likely to get Alzheimer's.

Centenarian

A person who has reached the age of 100. In the UK, the Queen sends out a special telegram to British citizens who celebrate their 100th birthday.

Dementia

Dementia is one of the main causes of disability in later life and mainly affects people over the age of 65. It can, however, affect younger people too; there are about 800,000 people in the UK with dementia, and of these over 17,000 people are under the age of 65. Symptoms of dementia include memory loss (particularly short-term, long-term memory generally remains quite good), mood changes (e.g. being more withdrawn) and communication problems.

Demographic changes (ageing population/ grey population)

Demographics refer to the structure of a population. We are currently experiencing an increase in our ageing population. People are living longer thanks to advancements in medical treatment and care. Soon, the world will have more older people than children. This means that the need for long-term care is rising.

Osteoporosis

Osteoporosis is a disease that causes bones to become brittle and prone to breaking. One in two women and one in five men over the age of 50 will break a bone, mainly because of osteoporosis. As we grow older our bone density decreases. Weight bearing exercise and a diet rich in calcium and minerals help to strengthen bones and reduce fragility.

Pension

When someone reaches retirement age, they are entitled to receive a regular pension payment from the government. This payment takes the place of a salary. Many people choose to pay into a private pension fund throughout their career, in order to save extra money for when they retire. Often, employers also pay into a pension fund for their employees. The State Pension Age is gradually increasing. The Pensions Act 2011 will see the State Pension Age for both men and women increase to 66 by October 2020 to 'keep pace with increases in longevity (people living longer)'.

Retirement

This is when a person leaves their job and stops working, usually because of age or ill health. Recently, people have made the decision to work for longer, being influenced by wanting to remain active in society and financial pressures.

Social care

Refers to non-medical care for the disabled, ill and elderly who find it difficult to look after themselves. Social care provides care, support and assistance to allow people to live their lives as fully as possible by helping them with everyday tasks they can't do on their own. This allows people to take part in an active lifestyle as some people may need help to live in their home, get washed and dressed or go out and about to meet friends.

Assignments

1. Create a presentation to perform in front of your class, explaining what happens as you age. See 'Are you ready? What you need to know about ageing' on page 3 for more information.

2. Problem drinking amongst the elderly is on the rise. To combat this, the Scottish Parliament wants to become the first EU country to have a minimum price for alcohol, which would be around 50p per unit. With this new price structure, a bottle of vodka that currently costs around £9 would be pushed up to £13. Researchers have said that an increase like this could save around 50,000 lives over the next ten years as many pensioners would not be able to afford the increase. Do you think this is a good idea? Do you think it will work? Discuss in small groups, and come up with some alternative solutions. See 'Elderly drinking is on the rise' on page 33 for more information.

3. Imagine you are a reporter for your local newspaper. You have been asked to write an article about social care services for the elderly. In your article you should explain what social care is, and be sure to address some of the current issues surrounding the topic. You might want to look at 'Care in crisis 2012' on page 20 and 'Social care: how it could be paid for in the future' on page 22, as well as any other newspaper articles about social care and care homes for inspiration.

4. Do some research about care homes. You could try looking at care home websites, or even visit one if you have the chance. Perhaps you already know someone in a care home, maybe you could ask them about their experience? Do you think you would enjoy living in a care home? Maybe they are nicer than you thought they would be. Maybe they are worse. Write a blog post describing your feelings and thoughts about care homes.

5. Research the laws surrounding the State Pension Age. Under the current guidelines, when will you be able to retire? You might find this website helpful: www.gov.uk/calculate-state-pension. What will you do to prepare for your retirement? When will you start? On one A4 side of paper, write some notes on the preparations you will take, and when you will put them into action.

6. 'The world will have more people who live to see their 80s or 90s than ever before.' Why is this? What are possible consequences of an ageing demographic? Is our ageing population a good thing? Or a bad thing?

7. In small groups, create a scheme that will teach older people how to make use of the Internet. What kind of things would you teach the elderly? How do you think they would benefit from using the Internet? How would you explain the concept of Facebook and setting up a profile to an older person? Design a leaflet explaining your scheme, what you will teach people and why.

8. Draw and describe a stereotypical old person. Compare your drawing with others and explain why you drew what you did. Now, draw and describe how you think people from an older generation see you. Look carefully at each drawing and discuss the idea of perceptions and stereotypes, and how these change with age. Is it harmful to discriminate against others because of their age?

9. Create an informative leaflet about dementia to be displayed at your local health centre. Be sure to include the symptoms of dementia, what causes dementia, who is most likely to be affected by dementia and what can be done to protect against dementia.

10. Depression is one of the most common illnesses affecting older people, with loneliness being a major factor: one in three over-65s in the UK want to be more socially active. To help overcome this, think of some activities to get the elderly more active and involved. Try to have these activities include both social and physical elements, such as dancing.

11. Your elderly neighbour Barbara is in a wheelchair and requires a lot of care. Her son visits her occasionally, but never stays very long. When he does come round you hear a lot of shouting and banging. You are worried that she is not being well cared for and possibly abused. What do you do?

12. Interview an older person of your choosing. Ask them about their life and experiences. Here are a few questions to get up started: Where did they grow up? Where did they work? What are their hobbies? Compile a report and present it to your group.

Acknowledgements

The publisher is grateful for permission to reproduce the following material.

While every care has been taken to trace and acknowledge copyright, the publisher tenders its apology for any accidental infringement or where copyright has proved untraceable. The publisher would be pleased to come to a suitable arrangement in any such case with the rightful owner.

Chapter One: Ageing trends

What is ageing? © Science Museum 2012, Are you ready? What you need to know about ageing © 2012 DementiaToday.com, Talkin' 'bout my generation © London Youth, UK performs poorly on experience of ageing © Mature Times, Older people are happier in Brazil and South Africa © 2004-2012 SquareDigital Media Ltd, Lesbian, gay and bisexual people in later life © Stonewall, Implementing a ban on age discrimination in the NHS – making effective, appropriate decisions © Crown copyright 2012, What is ageism? © Age UK Group, Ten priority actions to maximise the opportunity of ageing populations © United Nations Population Fund (UNFPA) and HelpAge, Does life begin again at retirement? © Campbell Harrison 2012.

Chapter Two: The cost of ageing

The dangers of our ageing population © Telegraph Media Group Limited 2012, Why our ageing population is an asset not a burden © 2012 AOL (UK) Limited, More than one in five pensioners at risk of poverty © Pensioners Campaign UK 2012, Pensioners in work doubled since 1993 © 2008-2012 Confused.com, Pension gap: a father's and son's tale © Telegraph Media Group Limited 2012, Care in crisis 2012 © Age UK Group, Social care: how it could be paid for in the future © Crown copyright 2011, Government to implement Dilnot care reforms 'as soon as it is able' © 1997-2012 Centaur Media Plc.

Chapter Two: Health issues

Age-related illnesses © 2012 mylastsong.com Ltd, Top ten tips for better ageing © Age UK Group, What is dementia? © 2012 Alzheimer's Society, Are you worried about dementia? © 2000-2012 YouGov plc, Depression in later years © The Grandparents' Association, Elderly drinking is on the rise © ANA Nursing 2012, Recognise and report elder abuse © Crown copyright 2012, About loneliness © 2012 Campaign to End Loneliness, Living alone 'raises death risk in elderly' © NHS Choices 2012, Can technology help us to support the ageing population? © Guardian News & Media Ltd 2012, One in three over-65s in the UK want to be more socially active © 2011-12 Mature Times.

Illustrations:

Pages 8 and 37: © Don Hatcher, page 3 and 33: © Simon Kneebone, pages 18 and 25: © Angelo Madrid.

Images:

Cover and page 5 © Druvo, page 11 © Kurhan, page 14 © Graham Acred, page 15 © James Cridland, page 17 © Rendery, page 21 © Mark Stay, page 27 © Jackie Staines, page 30 © thorbhorn kongshavn, page 35 © Jackie Staines, page 41 © Micah Burke.

Additional acknowledgements:

Editorial on behalf of Independence Educational Publishers by Cara Acred.

With thanks to the Independence team: Mary Chapman, Sandra Dennis, Christina Hughes, Jackie Staines and Jan Sunderland.

Cara Acred

Cambridge, January 2013.